to Sam —

FAST LINES

Hope you enjoy it!
All best wishes

STEWART ✕ Tyrrell - Ford ✕

ef

STEW

FORD

FAST LINES

Memorable Moments in
Motorsports by Pete Lyons from
VINTAGE RACECAR Magazine

Pete **Lyons**

octane press

octane press

Edition 1.1, August 2011

ISBN-10: 0-9829131-9-2
ISBN-13: 978-0-9829-1319-2

On the front cover:
Mario Andretti, Vel's Parnelli Jones VPJ-4, Monaco 1975

On the back cover:
(upper) Juan Manuel Fangio, Maserati A6GCS, at Thompson, CT, 1954;
(lower) Aston Martin DBR9 at Sebring, 2005

Book design by Tom Heffron
Copy edit by Charles Everitt

www.octanepress.com

Printed in the United States of America

For Lorna, whose idea this was.

Contents

Foreword

THE AUTOMOBILE, as we know it, is 125 years old and its racing history is just as long. Since the very first race, in 1895, countless writers, hacks, journalists, and scribes have held forth about auto racing in newspapers, magazines, books, and now on the Internet. In my humble opinion, only a handful of the writers who covered the more than 125 years of racing history have elevated motorsport journalism to a level of erudition worthy of the term "motorsport literature." The famed Denis Jenkinson is certainly one of those notable authors, and the gentleman whose collected writings for *Vintage Racecar* you hold in your hand is certainly another.

To this day, I still can't explain why Pete agreed to write for me, but I'll be forever thankful that he did! When I started a new magazine about the history and competition of historic racing cars, I wanted a respected name in motorsport journalism who could give *Vintage Racecar* instant credibility. Pete brought that in spades, with more than 30 years of experience covering Formula 1 and Can-Am for the likes of *Autosport, Racecar,* and *AutoWeek*.

During these past 14 years, Pete has written a monthly column for *Vintage Racecar* titled FASTLINES, which has covered everything imaginable from the long, illustrious history of motorsport and has done so—month in and month out—with intelligence and insight.

This compilation embodies a selection of Pete's favorite columns from this ever growing body of work, but with more than 150 gems to choose from, I don't know how he could have possibly chosen only 55 . . . they are all so good!

For everyone at *Vintage Racecar*, I hope you enjoy this fantastic look at the racing world . . . through the mind and eyes of Pete Lyons.

Casey Annis
Publisher/Editor
Vintage Racecar

Introduction

WHAT I HOPE YOU'LL ENJOY reading here is something like a starting grid of vintage race cars: an anthology of pre-owned magazine columns restored to run anew.

Appropriately, *Vintage Racecar* is the publication from which these stories are drawn. A premier monthly devoted to the history of auto racing, *VR* was launched in 1998 by Casey Annis, a reformed medical research scientist who accepted that his passion for motorsport was the greater and chose to pursue it as a publisher. Also as an editor, writer, marketer, and band-beater, even as his magazine's art director, early on. Not to mention igniter-of-the-spark and enforcer-of-the-deadline for people like me.

Casey greatly honored me with his invitation to become one of his original contributors. FASTLINES, a series of columns begun elsewhere years before, appeared in the very first issue of what then was called *Vintage Racecar Journal and Market Report* and has continued regularly throughout the ... gosh ... 14 volumes since.

Which means two things: our publisher has been uncommonly successful in a tough business, and that I've written ... wow ... a bunch of columns for him.

Too many to fit in a book of reasonable size. That called for the kind of painful culling that (I imagine) faces an organizer of vintage races who yearns to present more cherished machines than will fit on the track. But with pain can come gain; I found the pruning process instructive.

I came to columns after many seasons of turning out Sunday night race reports. That's a writing environment analogous to the race car cockpit itself, where deadline pressure forces you into a tight, noisy, frenetically fast little world in which you're trying to "drive the perfect race"— produce an accurate, informative, readable, saleable blend of all the incidents and results and impressions and news that make up an event weekend. You type it out and send it off and hope you got it mostly right.

Column-crafting, I discovered, is like going back to the track when all has fallen quiet. You stroll around, remembering, wondering, putting diverse observations together until, with luck, some new understanding forms in your mind.

Combining columns for this book carried that synthesis a step further. Each month, when you decide what to write about and how to write it, usually you think of the piece as standing alone, isolated from previous ones. But looking back through my body of *Vintage Racecar* work as a whole, I saw certain recurrent themes emerging.

Freedom is important to me, for example. So is adventure, fun, and honor. I admire warriors and their weapons. You may notice I love the music of racing engines.

But racing has a dark side. We enthusiasts have always wrestled with that, especially in my era, when drivers were always so close to gruesome death that I, for one, tried not to be too close to them. Too often, I failed. Mourning hurt. But, in the fashion of the day, one mouthed platitudes and went on to the next race.

Looking back, those seem very distant days, because racing today is so much safer. It's a huge change, but is it wholly positive? I've included some personal thoughts.

In terms of nuts-and-bolts, as hard as one tries to keep one's writing fresh month to month, I noted a tendency to reach for favorite words and phrases again and again. Lined up side by side, such repetitions are glaring. Also—I blush—there emerged spelling and/or grammatical errors, even passages that might been worded more clearly. In such instances I've played editor.

Thus not every sentence here is *precisely* the way it first appeared in the magazine. Sorry if that offends, but let me point out that a parallel can be drawn in the way vintage race cars are restored for further competition. You make them as strong as you can.

As always, my wonderful wife Lorna is an unseen tower of power behind this project. We met because of racing, she still enjoys racing as much as I do, and thus she is understanding of my preoccupation with racing and writing about it. I couldn't have raced through getting this book done without her. I am grateful, my love.

None of this did I ever foresee mumble-mumble years ago, when my dad, Ozzie Lyons, started taking me to sports car races on the East Coast, places like Bridgehampton, Lime Rock, Thompson, Sebring, and Watkins Glen. Mostly we went because it was novel and interesting and enjoyable, but as a photographer and writer Ozzie was sending stories to various publications, and he encouraged me to try my hand at it. That casually, race reporting became my career.

I can't imagine one I'd have enjoyed more. Following racing I've been to six continents and what must approach 200 motorsports venues; I've watched (and listened to!) some of history's most marvelous racing machines; I've met and, sometimes, become friends with many of the greatest competitors in what to me is the greatest of sports, always enthralling, exciting, fulfilling. I've managed to create some stories and pictures that pleased me, too.

Spend decades in race-watching and you accumulate a million rich experiences that cannot be crammed into race reports. As I remarked above, only later is there time to ponder and dig deeper and bring things together in your mind. Then one day, if you're really fortunate, an enthusiast named Casey Annis founds *Vintage Racecar* and offers you a virtual raceway to run it all again.

Thanks, Boss!

Learn more about the magazine at www.vintageracecar.com. To check out the author's other books, historic racing photos, calendars, and DVDs, visit www.petelyons.com.

Burned Bear, Denny Hulme at Mosport, 1970.

Section 1

Heroes

|

Sir Stirling Moss

Vintage Racecar, November 1998

STIRLING MOSS STILL moves like a busy man with a race to win. He bounces into the Watkins Glen media center bang on time, springs lightly onto the dais, and takes possession of a microphone with the same easy command he used to show in a Formula One car. His fresh white tennis shirt and shorts display how trim and tanned he keeps himself, and also provide him a quip to get this thing rolling.

"Excuse me for being in shorts," he says in those familiar clipped, laconic British tones. "When I started racing, you didn't even have to wear crash hats." The roomful of vintage race enthusiasts chuckles appreciatively, and we're off.

The old pro knows exactly what we want—him. So he throws in a deprecating little personal joke about his all-but-hairless scalp: "I look 'round at people my age and I'm appalled. Some of them are grey. I'm not." In the middle of a long story about a long race, he raises rueful titters with: "One thing you don't know when you're young is that when you get older they take out the long-range tank and put in the sprint tank."

Working his crowd with the instincts of a lounge comedian, when someone asks if he still does his famous handstands he replies, "No, I can't do some things I used to do, no . . . one just hopes that one can make up for it with sex."

Somebody else wants to know which drivers he most liked dueling with. "Slower ones," he snaps back.

Every *bon mot* brings a laugh. Every face in the room has a grin under shining eyes. This is better than they could have hoped for. This is Stirling Moss, legendary driver, fellow vintage racer, and accessible human being.

Motorsports fans of my generation and range of interest grew up with one name at the top of their personal pantheon. With Fangio retired, Stirling Moss was The Best in the World. Never mind that he never became World Champion, not quite; those who did were lucky to out-point him, and they knew it. Moss was The Master, the one who showed the world what a car could do, and what a driver could be. Smooth, stylish, utterly focused on winning, but gentlemanly about it, this man was the consummate motorsports professional—probably the first.

And how many former world-class drivers can you name who, at the age of nearly 69, still compete on an amateur level just for the fun of it?

That's why he's here on September 14-15, driving a Chevron B36 and a Lotus 23 in SVRA races celebrating the 50th birthday of this venue he helped make famous. It was Moss who brought international renown to The Glen by winning its 1959 *Formule Libre* event, and

Moss, F1 Cooper, lapping Midget at Watkins Glen, 1959.

whose enthusiasm for the place and the people helped bring the Grand Prix of the United States here from 1961 through 1980.

This year happens to mark Stirling's own 50th in the sport. His driving career hasn't been continuous, because of his near-fatal accident in 1962, but he's never left the scene. Today he frequently drives other people's historic cars, and has three of his own, another Lotus, a Lola, and a Mustang.

"Racing's always fun, because every car is different," he tells his rapt audience. "The pleasure is getting out there and learning new things, and trying to go faster. I still enjoy it, because it's a struggle. It's the greatest sport, to me, in the world.

"My threshold of fear has come a hell of a lot closer, I'll tell you that," he adds, getting another laugh. "I get shit-scared much faster."

Laugher, pleasure, enjoyment, fun ... these concepts keep recurring as Moss talks about racing. Somebody points that out, and wonders if Stirling thinks today's drivers have as much fun as he did. "No, I don't think fun comes into the equation. Some do enjoy the type of life they can have, and driving an F1 car to its limit is obviously exhilarating. But I think they miss out on the life around racing.

"It's a bit like my son, when he goes out dancing. There's bloody loud music and the girl stands two meters away and they shout at each other. In my day, you stood as close as you could and you tried to get her passionate."

Talk about Juan Fangio, he is asked. "I'm biased, I think he's the greatest driver the world's ever known. If one is talking of just sheer skill, probably Ayrton Senna was of that sort of skill, but as a man, as a person, Fangio was immaculate in the way he drove. [At Mercedes] we were known at the Train, because we were just together all the time, and I was only able to do that because of his style, his cleanness of driving. There's a lot of dirty drivers, I mean Jack Brabham would go over the edge and throw rocks at you. But Fangio would be exactly where he should be. He was an extremely ethical person."

Regrets? "I have no regrets now about not having won the World Championship. I mean the first year I lost it I was very upset. [Later]

I was a bit less upset. Providing you have the respect of your other drivers, it didn't worry me. Always in my life, the race that matters most to me is the race I'm in today. Because I can die today. I can get a bad reputation today. Whether it's a title race or not doesn't really affect the importance. Unfortunately now, because we have a World Championship, the race doesn't matter as much as the points it carries, and that, I think, is a shame.

"The thing I am sorry I didn't do is Indianapolis, because Indy really is an amazing event, a great occasion. I don't know that I would enjoy it or not, but I'm sorry I didn't do it. And I would like to have tried stock car racing and dragsters, because I think every niche of motor racing has its interest."

Where else but a vintage event would such memories and sentiments and, yes, humor flow so freely, so richly, so warmly?

Patiently, Moss answers every question as if it's the first time he's ever been asked, and when it's time to finish he makes a point of being

In Mille Miglia-winning Mercedes at VIR, 2004.

nice. "Thank you for your enthusiasm," he says, "and I hope everybody has as much fun here as I intend to."

Not a fan in the room doubts Stirling Moss is a true World Champion.

Sir Stirling continued to race with great enthusiasm for another 13 years, until he finally stepped out of the cockpit in the early summer of 2011 at the age of 81.

2

Mario Andretti:
Still the Champ!

Vintage Racecar, July 2003

ANYONE WHO SAW the terrifying tape of Mario Andretti's 200-mph "blowover" at Indianapolis on April 23 will easily visualize the same guy booting Duncan Dayton's Lotus 79 around Long Beach 11 days earlier. Happily, the historic F1 car came back unscathed. Whatever he's driving, Mario still loves to gas it.

Apparently he has trouble remembering he's 63. And who among us doesn't share that problem? Heck, I'm practically his age, and the very same day that Mario was executing his telegenic multiple backflip-cum-cartwheel at Indy, I was throwing karts around a track in Riverside—off the track, twice or thrice. So I'm nobody to tell people they're too old for anything they love to do.

How much Andretti loves race driving was plain on his face as he stood surrounded by TV lenses and microphones shortly after his Indy adventure. His voice still quavering but his eyes sparkling, he described how a car had crashed right in front of him and he ran straight over a piece of debris, which pitched his car's nose high enough to convert downforce to lift. His field of view went all sky-blue as the car whipped over backward like a speedboat run amok. It kept flipping in mid-air for what seemed like half an hour, he said. It finally crashed down in a spectacular, parts-shedding tumble that, incredibly, gave him nothing worse than a rap on the helmet.

What was going through his mind, someone wanted to know. "What the hell am I doing here!" he retorted with a laugh.

I thought the laugh expressed exhilaration as well as nervousness. I sensed he was feeling adrenaline, relief, and joy-of-life. I presume he's taken that heady brew many times before, and that it nourishes him. The drink of champions.

What happened at Long Beach was supposed to be a slow-speed exhibition of classic F1 cars by several former F1 drivers. They weren't going to wear helmets, so their grins could show, and they were only going to go two laps. The cars were loaned by members of Historic Grand Prix, the vintage organization that would be putting on a real race prior to the CART Champ Car round on Sunday. The demo was at lunchtime on Saturday, and included Emerson Fittipaldi in Steve Earle's McLaren M23, Bobby Rahal in a Wolf WR6, Pete Lovely driving his own Lotus 49, and several others—a stellar display.

The Lotus 79 was one of the very cars Mario had raced to his 1978 world driving championship, 25 action-packed years ago, and he also had recent experience with it. Less than three years before, he'd spent a day with Dayton and his crew at Watkins Glen, driving the glistening black-and-gold beauty for a *Road & Track Salon* (*R&T*, September 2000). At Long Beach, it must have fitted like skin.

"He asked for a helmet," Duncan Dayton chuckled, "so I handed him the one I've painted up just like his. He said, 'If I'm going to do this, I'm going to do it seriously, and I'm not gonna do no two slow laps. What can they do, throw me outta the joint?'"

And so as Bob Bondurant, Derek Daly, Parnelli Jones and company duly cruised onto the track, grinning and waving, the black-and-gold car with the silver-and-red helmet blasted away from them at full noise. At the end of two laps, as everyone else obediently turned back into the pits, Mario was on his third screaming, speedshifting run down Shoreline Drive.

I guess one could get all tut-tutty about such rules-flouting, but dammit, I cheered. Isn't exuberance what all this is about?

And the sight did bring memories flooding. Mario Andretti's career on track has been central to my own behind the guardrails, and I was an eyewitness to some of his championship-winning races in this landmark Lotus. I was even here in 1977 when he drove, not this car but its predecessor, the type 78, to victory in these streets. That victory by an American established the Long Beach Grand Prix as a major event in this country, while together the two Lotus models established ground effects in F1, thereby changing the very shape of racing worldwide.

At the moment of Mario's naughtiness on Saturday, I still had 23 hours before I needed to decide which one of the Historic Grand Prix teams would receive a cup with my name on it. The idea was to honor what I thought was the best effort at reviving the spirit of the days these cars used to race for real, here at Long Beach in particular.

But we had 27 of them! All beautiful! All superbly presented by owner-drivers who cherish them and revere their histories. I went around the HGP garage thinking, "I might as well throw a dart—it'll hit a winner."

In the end, it was a sheet of paper that tipped the balance. A job list lying atop a rear wing. There were other such sheets with other cars, but this one riveted me. It called for actions such as HIGHER SECOND GEAR and FRONT RIDE HEIGHT DOWN ONE QUARTER. There were eight or nine such tasks, all meant to make the car faster. I thought, "These guys are serious!" and, "This is how it used to be!"

It meant something, too, that a world champion was so confident about the old machine's preparation that he was willing to boot it hard.

Sunday mid-day, while everyone was feeling good about a truly rousing HGP Grand Prix, I announced my choice for the cup. Everyone deserved it, I tried to emphasize, but this weekend at this place my eye kept coming back to one car and its team; a car of great historical significance that was beautifully presented and driven with great spirit. So to honor the outstanding work of crewmen Greg Elliff, Jim Bascetta, and Joe Hatch, I called on Duncan Dayton.

And I'd have gone that way even if Mario hadn't done that third lap—honest!

3

Jimmy Clark

Vintage Racecar, June 2008

BY COMPELLING COINCIDENCE, the Editor's deadline for this issue fell 40 years to the day after our world lost one of its most brilliant talents. Thus I am moved to add my few words to the torrent of appreciation that has been appearing about the great Jim Clark.

Let me hasten not to claim I knew him. The nearest I ever came were the outskirts of pit road conversations here and there, back when my ears were young enough to overhear, but I was too young to dare intrude.

So I'll have to rely on what I saw of his dazzling ability in a racing car, and what others have said about his iridescent personality.

One of my best memories is of standing stark naked—I mean there was no protective barrier in those days—on the very apex of the old 90-degree downhill bend at Watkins Glen and witnessing Clark overcook it.

I suppose he was feeling out the latest possible braking point. Through my viewfinder I saw his tiny green missile of a Lotus come whistling in toward me, just as it had on previous laps, but this time it was running a bit wider from my toes than before. A matter of two feet, maybe.

Precisely as I noticed, I also saw Clark notice. I saw white flashes as his eyes went wide. Whirling, I watched . . . nothing. Whatever he did to adjust, it was too subtle for me to catch. The car simply tracked on around and left the turn in full-bore, screaming acceleration.

I daresay for him the incident was so minor that minutes later he wouldn't have remembered. I've never forgotten.

Possibly it was that same October weekend that I stood listening to Clark talking with his leader at Lotus, Colin Chapman, about the car's behavior through another turn, the long, fast sweeper at the south end. I gathered he was having trouble holding a smooth arc because the steering wasn't giving enough information. "It's so light," I heard Jimmy say.

Colin simply nodded, as if to imply, "I know, that's how I build them." Not many seasons later the conversation would have turned to front-end downforce, but I doubt even Chapman foresaw that then.

What I took away was a sense of awe: that exquisite little F1 Lotus was so delicate, it taxed even the great Jim Clark's superb sensitivity.

That's how we thought of him. He was not superhuman, really, but he showed us just how super a human could be. He was one of those rare racing drivers who elevate our comprehension of racing, our appreciation, our wonderment. We can be proud of our sport if people like him are involved.

Another small, indelible moment: Canadian GP at Mosport, in rain that has everybody tiptoeing along the pit straight in flumes of spume. Right opposite the Lotus pit, Clark gives a deliberate stab of gas. The rear tires break into wild spinning. Clark's head is turned straight at Chapman, the message clear: "D'you see? See what I'm copin' with out here?"

A little of what I missed by never knowing him personally has been filled in by people who did. Dan Gurney, for instance, who was very close as both teammate and competitor, one whom many put on a level with Clark. Of many things that bubble up in Dan's mind about Jimmy, one is this: how much fun the two had racing Lotus Cortina sedans together.

"Some people aren't willing to put their reputation at risk by jumping into something that they don't have any background on, and Jimmy wasn't that way at all. I admired him for that," Gurney remarked. "Jimmy would have loved a Trans-Am car."

As I'm sure he loved driving big sports racing cars (though Lotus's wasn't a good one) and Indy 500 cars (Chapman built him a winner).

Another insight is from long-time racing PR man Rod Campbell, who tells of making many transatlantic phone calls to Jimmy's flat in Paris, trying to entice the twice F1 World Champion and 1965 Indy 500 winner to attend a year-end charity gala in Montreal. Rod recalls that Jimmy finally agreed, but only on condition he needn't speak.

"Once he was there, of course, we convinced him he had to say something. And his little speech was an absolute highlight, the best of everybody's. He was a really smart guy, and his jokes were really, really funny. His sense of timing was superb. We'd never seen that side of him at the races."

Someone else once told me of being at a racing party and noticing Jimmy walk in. "He looked around the room, spotted the prettiest girl there, went straight over to her, chatted her up and cut her out of the herd and left with her, just like that." My confidant's voice was full of the same dazed admiration I felt when I watched Clark handle a racing car.

Too few times, alas.

4

Briggs Cunningham

Vintage Racecar, October 2003

FIFTY YEARS AGO, in 1953, an American-made Cunningham sports racing car won the second-ever Sebring 12-hour race. Then Briggs Swift Cunningham's team carried the blue-and-white competition colors of the USA to the 21st 24 Hours of Le Mans, earning third place overall and first in class.

"Mr. C." died this July. We don't have space here for all the things that should be said about him, but I do want to acknowledge his racing achievements and also his manner of going racing. These things were foundation stones for my own enthusiasm.

Though I came to the sport just too late to have personal memories of Cunningham's bold, burly cars in serious action, my father brought home pictures and stories of them from his racing photo safaris. These images defined a sort of starting point for my conception of what sports cars ought to be.

Here were all-American interpretations of the exotic European theme. Daring marriages of brute Detroit horsepower with agile chassis. Hot-rods with road manners.

And an American team taking on the world's elite.

Peering through the long lens of history, I think it's hard to get Cunningham and his colleagues in proper focus. It is tempting, now, to over-glamorize their quest. In fact, how many of their

American contemporaries, nation-wide, would have understood what they were doing, or would have cared? On the other hand, given half a century of hindsight, today we could easily dismiss their vehicles as primitive.

But I feel genuine value and honor in what they attempted, and given their times and circumstances, I find their effort breathtakingly sophisticated.

Briggs Cunningham was born to enormous wealth, and his ambitions and standards were those of a dedicated sportsman. Apart from his love of automobiles, he was a "Corinthian" yachtsman who once commanded his own sailboat to a successful defense of the America's Cup. In wartime, having tried to enlist but been turned away because he was overage, he served his nation by supplying an amphibious plane for coastal submarine and rescue patrol, complete with himself as pilot.

Cunningham was so placed in life that he would have been perfectly able to consume cars of others. But he chose to create ones of his own.

The roots of the Cunningham cars reach back to the 1930s, when Briggs was active with fellow fans of European sports cars in a group called the Automobile Racing Club of America (ARCA), a forerunner of the postwar SCCA. Young Briggs didn't race at that time, in deference to his mother's concern, but he owned numerous cars and let friends race them. In 1936 a Cunningham MG was borrowed for Le Mans, though Briggs didn't go over himself.

ARCA members were not snobs about their machinery, and several happily built "specials," European cars stuffed full of American power. In 1939 Briggs, a former Yale engineering student, commissioned a blend of attributes he admired from both sides of the Atlantic. Dubbed the BuMerc, it was a Buick chassis with the straight eight engine repositioned rearward and hopped up. The body came from a crashed Mercedes SSK. The BuMerc was meant for street driving, but in a 1940 ARCA event called the Worlds Fair Grand Prix one of Briggs's friends was holding second until he crashed.

In 1948, with his mother now gone, Briggs himself drove the BuMerc to second place in the first Watkins Glen race. At age 41, Cunningham launched his racing career in earnest, driving a British-made Healey Silverstone powered by a Cadillac V-8. He also drove a Cadillac-engined '53 Ford—a "Fordillac"—both on the street and in time trials. It clocked 105 mph on Daytona Beach. Briggs got an idea. How about entering this all-American Fordillac in the famous Le Mans race he'd heard so much about?

Stuffy Le Mans officials replied that Monsieur Cunningham would be welcome at La Sarthe, but not with some mongrel car. He must race a properly branded production vehicle.

So Briggs duly turned up at the Sarthe in 1950 with a team of two Cadillacs, one a stock two-door sedan, the other a chassis wearing a special low-drag body built with the help of Grumman aircraft engineers. This "Le Monstre" placed 11th after Briggs himself had to dig it out of a sandbank. The sedan cruised home 10th.

His fire well lit, later that year Briggs set up the B.S. Cunningham Company near his winter home in West Palm Beach. Running this small factory were the partners responsible for the Fordillac, mechanical genius Bill Frick and brilliant driver and sound businessman Phil Walters, who raced midgets as "Ted Tappett." Working flat-out, they and a small staff of gifted craftsmen produced a prototype Cunningham C-1 street car (with a Cadillac engine) and then a trio of C-2R racers (powered by the new Chrysler Hemi) just barely in time for Le Mans 1951.

For five hours on Sunday morning, a brand new, all-American Cunningham held second place in the world's most important sports car race.

Engine problems knocked that car back to 18th at the end, while crashes took out its two sisters. But Cunningham was legitimately encouraged. He sent the C-2Rs out on the U.S. sports car circuit, where John Fitch won two races and became the first SCCA national champion. The image of those glistening white roadsters with the bold blue stripes was burned into every American sports car fan's soul. So was this born gentleman's sportsmanlike approach to the sport.

That's where I came in. Today, I wonder what shape sports car racing would have taken in this country without Briggs Cunningham. Would some other champion have stepped forward to fly our colors in Europe? Would Reventlow have been inspired to build his Scarabs? Hall and Sharp their Chaparrals? Gurney his Eagles? Ford their GTs?

We can't know. But we do know Mr. C. led the way.

5

Mark Donohue in F1

Vintage Racecar, May 2004

FRIDAY EVENING BEFORE the 1975 Austrian Grand Prix, over a small dinner in a quiet countryside hotel, Mark Donohue told us about setting a 221-mph speed record the week before with his old Can-Am Porsche. "It's the only thing I've accomplished this year," he remarked with a small grin.

By his high standards, Mark's first full season in Formula 1 had been disappointing. He'd put in several strong, aggressive drives, but for midfield places. The Penske PC-1 car had handled badly and broken often, and Mark had made driving errors. His best finishes were a couple of fifths. Overall, it was not the performance we were used to seeing from Mark Donohue and Roger Penske, an already legendary partnership that had mastered almost every other form of racing.

As realistic as he was sensitive, Mark knew that most people in F1, even many involved with him, believed he didn't have the driving ability to win Grands Prix. Mark would talk of this, not easily but not shrinking from it. "I wouldn't have come back and said I'd do this if I didn't believe I could get the job done," he would say.

But at 38, he was aware of time running out. "I've always been on a year-to-year basis, and I don't know if I'll be asked to drive again next year."

Like so many stories in what has been called "the cruel sport," Mark's first experience of F1 had promised more. That was back in 1971, when Penkse made a deal with McLaren and entered Donohue— freshly famous as that year's Indy 500 champion—in the last two GPs of the season in Canada and the US. Mark took the challenge seriously, spending two weeks testing with the factory team in England, then testing some more on both North American tracks. But he couldn't get the McLaren to handle. An early M19, it had innovative "rising-rate" suspension linkages that worked in mysterious ways. In qualifying at Mosport he turned in only an average time.

Then on race day it rained. Mark Donohue finished third in his rookie GP.

Characteristically, he wasn't pleased with this remarkable result. As he wrote later in his book, *The Unfair Advantage*, the rain had been "a blessing that saved me from terrible embarrassment." But neither was he intimidated by the F1 regulars. "They didn't seem so fast to me. No one ever passed me."

His plans for the USGP were foiled by a rain-delayed Indy car race elsewhere, which took priority. Mark did spend time at Watkins

Monaco, 1975.

Glen, however, helping stand-in driver David Hobbs, and there he found fans encouraging him to continue in F1.

He wrote, "That was the first time I realized how much enthusiasm there was for American drivers to compete against the Europeans. Of course, [Mario] Andretti was driving for Ferrari and [Peter] Revson was in a third Tyrrell for the Watkins Glen race, but the comments seemed aimed toward me . . . my ego was really pumped up."

Busy with many other programs, Donohue didn't pursue F1 then. But only months after announcing his retirement in 1973, he pulled his driver's suit back on to lead Penske's 1974 plunge into F1.

It was one of three American efforts in a time that now seems halcyon. Don Nichols' Shadow was already established. Paralleling Penske as a newcomer team was Vel's Parnelli Jones with Andretti. Their car, the VPJ-1, joined the scene along with Donohue in the Penske Cars PC-1 for the '74 Canadian GP, again at Mosport.

By then I'd been covering F1 for two years, and was thrilled by what I called "the glistening presence" of the new entries. I wrote in *Autosport*, "Both machines, and indeed both teams, looked as superbly finished as everyone had expected. The sheer quality of the dual American effort made even the best prepared of the Europeans look suddenly aware of their season-battered age."

Unfortunately, results didn't come up to looks. Both there and at the Glen, Donohue had niggling new-car problems which robbed him of time to show his stuff as a chassis tuner. In Canada he qualified 24th of 26, and finished 12th. (Andretti started 16th, finished seventh.) In the USGP, Mark improved his starting place to 14th, but dropped out with broken suspension. (Andretti qualified an electrifying third, but the Parnelli failed at the start.)

During 1975 Mark lived in England near the Penske shop, working full-time both on the car and on making himself a GP driver. At the opening race in Argentina, I wrote, he looked "tougher and leaner and browner than ever before." The PC-1, however, "was visibly the worst-handling car on the track." Mark did manage to come home seventh.

Over the next several races there wasn't much improvement, except for a points-paying fifth in Sweden. But that was a place behind Andretti. Putting pride aside, Penske let Donohue try out a March 751. Much smoother and steadier, was the driver's report. "It's sensitive to tuning—when you do something, you can feel the difference; it's easy to drive; it's got the right aerodynamic properties; it's simple, and it's light." Mark duly drove a March in the British GP at Silverstone, the tenth round of the year. He scored his second fifth-place there, although he was in the fence, one of numerous drivers who crashed because of a sudden rain squall that ended the race early. The brand-new 751 chassis had to be rebuilt.

Next race was the German GP at the Nürburgring, where loose stones punctured many tires. The second time one of his fronts went flat in the race, Mark parked.

Then came Austria's fast, swooping Oesterreichring, one more track neither American newcomer had seen before. Donohue took a grid position next to Andretti on the tenth row. But during Sunday morning's warm-up session Mark had another front tire go flat at high speed. The March slid into the catch fences that were all the rage in those days and the chain-link wadded up under it, lifting it over a low guardrail into a billboard. Mark's helmet impacted a steel post.

At first it looked OK. He was awake and talking. But he mentioned a severe and worsening headache. Airlifted to a hospital, he underwent surgery for hemorrhaging in the brain. He died two days later.

It hit me very hard. Revson had been killed only the year before, and Donohue had seemed at least as close a friend. Days earlier he'd taken me boating. When the news came I was in the middle of writing something about how wonderful racing is. It was difficult to finish the silly story. Not only had I greatly liked and admired Mark as a person and a racer, I'd been immensely proud of having fellow Americans in F1. I'd been rooting for Donohue to struggle up his learning curve and get to the top, where I was so used to seeing him.

I think, too, I shared his hope that he would finally show the doubting world that the scientific methods he'd applied to all his other racing cars would work in F1 as well.

But earlier that summer he'd told me the hectic pace of F1 was tough for him. "In American racing, we always seem to have plenty of time to set the car up, all day if we need it. Here we've got two and a half hours today, and two and a half hours tomorrow, and that's it. The other people seem to be able to cope with that; they know the circuits and they have a lot of experience with the cars and you can see them going fast right away."

Mark, whose whole career was based on a methodical application of laboriously discovered principles of vehicular dynamics, was not the sort of driver to simply jump into a car and scald lap records out of it. He did have driving ability aplenty, and there were occasions in the past when he had to show it. But it wasn't the way he thought it should be done.

He tried to approach F1 as he had approached so many other kinds of racing over the years, with patience, understanding, and logic. "It's a matter of the combination," he'd say. He wanted to get all the elements in the equation right first; success must automatically follow.

One of the peculiarities of F1 that frustrated him, though, was that F1 tires wouldn't behave as he expected on a skid pad. For years he'd used this circular patch of asphalt to establish a car's basic handling characteristics, to make adjustment upon painstaking adjustment to the chassis until it was all working in harmony under steady-state cornering conditions. But in F1 that didn't work. "Tires I'm used to will come up to operating temperature and stay there. But these tires just get hotter and hotter on the pad, and you can't get the car to settle down."

Therefore all his development had to be carried out on a race track, and almost always it had to be carried out amidst the pressures of a GP weekend. And it all had to be done by him. The team was compact, and on Donohue's shoulders were the double mantles of driver and engineer. He would have to drive at F1 tempo, and then switch his mind to cool contemplation. It took time to do this even when things were going well, and when they weren't he had nobody but himself to keep track of what path he was taking. His crew could keep a record of what he did to the car, but they couldn't be expected to always follow his train of thought. Thus when he went down a blind alley, it was he alone who had to find his way back out.

So Mark, so very concerned with appearances, was not "looking good." He was suffering through a bad patch, with not a lot of help. He was no stranger to this kind of situation, and had come through it before. In fact he had brought this upon himself, with his experienced eyes open. The greatest sorrow about his death was that it forever robbed him of his chance to bring it right in the end.

Mourning him, I wrote something about finding some meager consolation in knowing he voluntarily came back from retirement. The man needed to race. And, I said, "He knew what he was doing, he was no stranger to the violence of what could happen when the laws of physics by which he ruled his career turned against him. He had spent months in painful recovery from [a Can-Am crash]. If ever a racing driver understood the full, coldly scientific implications of what racing is about, it was Mark Donohue."

Nevertheless, I continued, in racing he found "the same sort of glee as a boy with a new toy; it is, after all, this same impetus that has driven Man to advance the mechanical arts since he came down from trees. Donohue with his record-breaking car was as one with his ancestor who devised a way of making fire. Living within Mark was the whole reason for human advancement."

Cold comfort for losing him. But it's what we had.

6

Chris Economaki:
Who Was
Grampa Gritzback?

Vintage Racecar, **September 2004**

THE HAPPY DRIVER you see here is *not* Henry Gritzback, aka "Grampa."
How I came to know that is a minor detective story I hope you'll enjoy.

My dad's photo archive includes several thousand 4x5-inch
negatives, many of which depict his lifelong enthusiasm for racing.

"Loose" at Altamont, NY, 1938.

According to Ozzie's notes on the paper neg sleeves, he took the earliest shots in 1938. Others are dated post-WWII. On one envelope he penciled a name, "Grampa Gritzback," and gave the location as Altamont, New York. His date is imprecise, "circa 1950."

All these action-packed images interest me for themselves, but the fact that none of the others were singled out for name-identification aroused my curiosity. Who was Gritzback? A long-forgotten hero of the age? Had I stumbled upon a treasure?

I already knew that this Altamont track, not to be confused with the Northern California venue of the same (notorious) name, was not far from my family's roots in the Albany-Schenectady area of Upstate New York. A quick online search—how my dad would have enjoyed the power of the Internet!—confirmed that Altamont, New York, is just to the west of Albany and still boasts a fairground to this day.

What's more, the Internet turned up several mentions of a Henry Gritzback, sometimes spelled Gritzbach, who was racing in that area in the immediate pre- and post-war period. But I couldn't find much beyond that.

When technology fails, turn to human beings. Let's see: who do I know with an encyclopedic recall of American auto racing?

"Hank Gritzback? Yessss... Hank Gritzback was from Schenectady, and he was what we called a 'third-heat driver.' See, in those days..."

Chris Economaki, veteran race announcer and reporter, founder of *National Speed Sport News*, still has the quick mind of youth. I ran into him on the green lawns of Bill Warner's Amelia Concours, and remembered to ask about my mystery driver. Without an instant's hesitation, Chris began telling me about county fair racing in the 1930s.

"The east was a highly populous place, and once the fair season began, late June through mid-October, there were a lot of races to go to and you could race every weekend and make some money," Economaki explained. "In Altamont, New York, the fair there is called the Tri-County Fair, and the closing day of the fair was auto race day. And it was big stuff, the only race a year of consequence in the Albany area. Guys would tow from all over.

"They'd qualify, and then the heat races were for six cars apiece. The fastest six qualifiers started in the first heat, and the top three finishers moved to the main event. The first three finishers of the second heat lined up fourth, fifth, and sixth in the main event. The third heat ran

Heat race at Altamont; man at mic *might* be Economaki.

the same way, and that's the area of Gritzback's expertise. He was a third-heat driver.

"The consolation race was for everybody that was left, and sometimes it had 20 or 25 cars, and the winner made the main event for a 10-car field. Guys would come for years and never make a main event. Gritzback made a few, but he was not a consistent main event runner. Nice old guy. Yeah . . ."

Well, according to the 'net, nice old Hank was a main event winner at least once, in 1953 at a New York track called Sydney Speedway. But obviously I hadn't uncovered a major star.

Still, I was enthralled to hear more about a time and a kind of racing I knew hardly at all. Chris obligingly took me back to the kindling of his own enthusiasm in 1932, when at the age of 13 he walked into a barber shop in his home town of Ridgewood, New Jersey, and spotted a photo of a racing car on the wall. The excited youngster soon found out the driver was the barber's son. Next time they went racing, Economaki went along.

Chris Economaki with Stirling Moss, Road America, 1967.

"Understand that this was a *huge* country then. Philadelphia was 90-some miles from Ridgewood, and *nobody* had ever traveled that far. Here I was going off to faraway places. Incredible.

"We'd get to the race track, and what are they gonna do with a 13-year-old? Hand me a bucket, 'Go get water.' And at fairgrounds the running water was only way over *there* someplace, in a *barn* somewhere. I'd go get the water and fill up the radiator and wipe the windshield. It was *my car* that I was taking care of, you know?"

And "his" driver, Bob Sall, went on to be the 1933 Eastern AAA champion.

"It was a great era," Chris continued. "There was no money in those days. No money. And yet everybody got to the next race somehow. Well, you were addicted. You made it happen. I went to a race in August of 1932 at Langhorne, Pennsylvania, when 101 cars qualified. Every one of 'em was homemade."

Chris mentioned that in later years, Altamont was one of the tracks where he called races. When I got home, I pulled out my father's photos with renewed interest. At last I knew who Hank Gritzback was.

But now I spotted a detail I'd missed before. The negative inside the "Grampa" envelope has "Jim Forte" hand-written just below the car.

The plot thickens! Back to Google. Yes, there was also a Jimmy Forte racing in that period. From the number 40 on the car in question, plus the nickname "Sporty" scrawled on the tail, it's pretty clear who this photo actually shows. The envelope was simply mislabeled.

Mistakes lead to learning. Thanks to this one, and to Chris Economaki's kindness, a window has opened for me onto something that obviously meant a lot to my dad. By the time I came along, so had sports cars and road racing, and that's the direction I went. But in the time and place of Ozzie's youth, if you wanted to race, you had to go to the local fairground. The dirt tracks really are the cradles of American auto racing.

Going by my dad's pictures, and Chris Economaki's marvelous memory, I missed a good time.

7

Juan Manuel Fangio: El Maestro

Vintage Racecar, August 2008

FIFTY-ONE YEARS after his fifth and final world championship, Juan Manuel Fangio is still my favorite F1 driver. Never mind that I never actually saw him race an F1 car, not for real. I believe I know what I would have seen.

That's because I grew up feasting on stories about him. Though I lacked the luck to witness any of his Grands Prix (I did see him win at Sebring in a sports car), it was my fortune to discover racing in the years when everyone who knew anything about my new passion deemed Fangio the best.

Yes, I was just an impressionable youth. But that type of impression sticks. And nothing I've heard since changes my feeling.

In everything said and written about Fangio by people who did know and watch him, what stands out is not only his utter mastery of the GP car of his time, but his timeless qualities as a human being.

Our Internet age makes it easy to read volumes about Fangio. Do a simple search and along with accounts of his incredible accomplishments you'll find words applied to him such as "grace," "nobility" and "sense of honor."

On formula1.com, Gerald Donaldson says Fangio's "generosity of

Fangio sets his own tire pressures before opening the new track at Thompson, CT, 1954.

spirit, sense of fair play, invariable courtesy, surprising humility and sheer humanity were universally praised and appreciated, especially by his peers. 'Most of us who drove quickly were bastards,' [said] Stirling Moss, who called him 'Maestro' and said he loved Fangio like a father."

Steve Barber, writing on jmfangio.org (click on the English button), notes that, "While other drivers might act like flamboyant prima donnas, Fangio was quiet and gentlemanly."

My own understanding and appreciation of the great man was formed chiefly by the words of Denis Jenkinson, the most inspirational journalist of my experience. My original 1959 copy of his immortal book, *The Racing Driver*, has been well-thumbed over the past 49 years, and I've just been going through it again, looking up lines that inspired me when I was young.

Page 31: "Fangio is the perfect example of this 'will to win' and it is evident the moment he gets in a Grand Prix car. His objective when practice starts is to record the fastest practice lap, and it is during split-second battles for this honor that you are most likely to see him at his best."

Page 54: "Fangio's ability to go fast with a broken car is truly remarkable, and two classic occasions stand out: one in the Mille Miglia when he finished second in an Alfa Romeo that had a broken steering connection, and the other at Spa when he won the Belgian Grand Prix with a Maserati that had broken its front spring mountings and was sagging at the front."

It's Jenkinson's chapter "Oversteer" that most excited me then and I find it still does. Some of the wingless F1 cars of the day were intentionally designed to break their rear tires loose at the limit, with the expectation that the driver would save the situation with a judicious application of power, providing there was enough. In Jenks's words, "In 1957 the 250F Maserati became amenable to this power technique . . . and throughout the season Fangio gave some wonderful demonstrations of cornering with the rear wheels held on breakaway . . . by using the throttle.

"I watched him closely on the bend before the pits at Rouen, which was fast and smooth and ideal for this technique, and you could see the car increasing its attitude angle . . . and then at the crucial moment he would apply power and hold the car in a long slide through the corner . . ..

"On a few occasions I saw him overdo this application of power and the tail snaked viciously, demanding instantaneous steering correction and in lesser hands the car would have spun round."

How I longed to see such artistry with my own eyes!

My father did meet the man. Ozzie photographed Sebring when Fangio drove there in 1954 and again in 1956, and also went to Thompson, Connecticut, when Fangio did some publicity laps. On another occasion my dad happened to be in a restaurant and noticed the world champion stroll in.

"He was all alone," I remember Ozzie telling me, "and he was looking around the room with almost a forlorn look on his face. He didn't really know me, but on impulse I jumped up and threw my arms apart and said, 'Fangio!' He lit up and came right over."

My dad had dinner with Juan Manuel Fangio.

I blew my one chance to even stand near him. It was just before a British GP at Silverstone, and I had broken off from my last-minute beavering on the grid to trot up to Copse corner to shoot the start. On the way I passed a small group of official-looking gentlemen, one of whom seemed vaguely familiar. "Huh," I said to myself. "That bloke looks like Fangio." Impossible, of course, and I hastened on.

Five minutes later the Tannoy announced a pleasant surprise: today the starting flag would be dropped by a special guest, the great Juan Manuel Fangio.

But a few years later, at Long Beach, I did manage a tiny personal interaction. It was the year Fangio came to drive an historic F1 Mercedes in a short demonstration race, and I climbed an amazingly empty TV tower to watch.

It was like all the old film had come to life: his brown leather helmet, the wind flapping the collars of his yellow polo shirt up on his neck, his bare, brawny arms working the wheel. As the magic few minutes ended and the Silver Arrow came into sight on its cool-off lap, way up atop my tower I threw my hands over my head and clapped them together to express my enthusiasm and gratitude.

Fangio spotted me. I saw his face light up.

8

A Fast Ride
with Dan Gurney

Vintage Racecar, July 2001

DAN GURNEY ONCE tried to show me how to wring the neck of a recalcitrant race car to squeeze out that last tenth of a second, and I blew it. The lesson, I mean. Couldn't take in a thing . . . except something important about Dan Gurney.

You don't get a lot of chances like this. Even when you make a career of race-camp-following, as I've done, not every day brings a whirl around a raceway with a master. Sure, it does happen, but it's surprisingly rare. Thirty-plus years I've been doing this, and I haven't scored close to 30 really fast rides.

That's why I'm still annoyed with myself for harboring some weird mental block the evening Gurney took me around Firebird in a Supra.

He was still on good terms with Toyota then, and had come to lend some luster to a press launch. When he started giving hot laps, I got into line quick. The Arizona sun was down as, finally, I buckled in alongside this towering man who has been a legend in this sport for nearly as long as I've known about it. "Hi," I said.

"Tell me how fast we're going," he replied.

Ah, he was glancing at my watch. So, obediently, as we completed our second tire-howling lap I pressed the button and shouted the

number at him. Call it 1:35.5, or something. He nodded, and bore
down. Next lap, new number: 1:35.8.

He frowned. No, he scowled. His lips got thin. I took a fresh
handful of grab bar.

It was one of the rides of my life. Or should have been. As the dusk
grew deeper, that screaming Supra seemed to be setting Firebird afire.
That poor screaming Supra. What a whipping it was getting. Redline
everywhere. Fists two blurs on the wheel. Shifts slamming through in
milliseconds, pedals all banging the floor. The brakes must be orange-
hot, I was thinking. The tires must be grinding down to the cords. My
neck was aching from all the pitching and heeling and yanking.

I did manage to notice one finer point of technique. In one tight little right-hander, Dan was starting the acceleration phase much earlier than I anticipated. My idea would have been to slide the back tires around, artfully holding opposite lock all the way through.

Well, to hell with art, on the track it's a time-waster. Dan was planting those tires and launching straight out, hard. Ah-hah.

"What's the time!" he demanded every lap. My answers weren't pleasing him. The numbers were still like 35.7, 35.9, 35.8. Ooooh, this poor car, I was thinking. It's too nice a car to treat like this. The whole thing must be on the point of meltdown. No way was he going to make it go faster. I had no fear, not a hint of it, but I was feeling the machine's pain big time.

It was going through my mind—I confess it—to give a false reading, just to get him to stop beating on this pitiable vehicle.

I didn't. Didn't have to. "Hey, 1:35.4!" I was able to announce, truthfully. That big, famous grin split that magazine-cover face, and he turned into the pits.

Self-recriminations began churning even as I was pulling off my helmet. I had just been riding with genius. I had been granted a glimpse into the heart of an art that has been a compelling mystery to me for practically all of my life. Dan Gurney personally had shown me how to shave down a lap time.

And I had missed the whole thing. I have no idea what he did differently on that last lap.

What I did come away with, though, was a renewed understanding of the man himself. Competitive? Sheesh. If you want to know what sort of mentality it takes to be a real racer, hang out with Big Dan.

There was the time in his office, where I'd gone to interview him, but he wanted to play. On his desk was one of those executive toys, a sort of plastic egg with a ball bearing inside. You were supposed to grip it in one hand, start up a cranking motion, and see how fast you could get the ball speeding around. The whirring sound told the rpm.

I proved to be no challenger to the Gurney best, and the interview was proceeding well until somebody else came in, casually picked up the egg, and started making whirring sounds.

Dan's eyes went to the egg. The pitch kept rising, rising . . . I'd lost my man. His long arm whipped out, snatched back the damn device, and he literally bent over it, tendons straining, face reddening, trying, trying, trying to get his rev record back. And he did.

When you do get to talk with Dan, you hear words like honor and pride. They are meaningful words to this man. He feels his nationality to the core. One of the magazines once did a cover story on him, and the blurb read "The Obsolete American." I couldn't argue with it. Remember that campaign by another magazine to get Gurney elected President? Still seems like a good idea to me.

Unlike a politician, though, Dan listens to what you say and returns a thoughtful, pertinent answer. Not necessarily a "correct" one, but honest. Once I remarked to him about how appalled I had been to see crowds on the very edge of the Grand Prix track in Mexico City.

Why should I feel that way, he demanded sharply. Hadn't I told him of my delight in being allowed a photographer's access to just such a hazardous position at Watkins Glen? (I had.) Then why would I wish to deny such a thrill to my fellow enthusiasts? (I won't again.)

Dan Gurney is the Le Mans winner who recounted to me, chuckling, how he'd run across the track, jumped in the car and took off without bothering about his seat belts. He did them up later, out on the Mulsanne Straight, once he'd got into top gear, steering with his knees . . . .

What do you suppose you could have learned riding along with him that day?

There's a lot of talk going through the US racing world about how to get Americans involved in F1 again. Dan's own son Alex is running one of the ladder classes in Europe right now, and my heartfelt good wishes to him. But he's got some big memories to fill. It has to be proven to me that they still make drivers like his dad.

Alex Gurney went on to be a major force in Grand-Am endurance racing, winning two Daytona Prototype championships as of July 2011.

9

Graham Hill:
Heroes are Human Too

Vintage Racecar, May 2006

FORTY MEMORIAL DAYS ago, I sat in the Indianapolis grandstand and witnessed Graham Hill capturing the second of the three crowns that still make him unique: he's the only driver ever to win the 500 (in 1966), the F1 world championship (in both 1962 and 1968) and Le Mans (1972).

As a "foreign" race driver, Hill was absolutely captivating to us Americans in those naive days. Tall, well-built from his competitive rowing, and as dashing as any classic English film star, he also possessed a dry (and often dirty) wit capable of convulsing whole dinner parties. On both sides of the "pond" he was a beloved figure to people who liked him personally and deeply respected his hard-knocks accomplishments.

Did you realize (I confess I didn't until digging through the literature just now) that Norman Graham Hill, auto racing champion, was 24 before he first drove an automobile of any kind???

He earned so little as a young technician with Smiths Instruments that he could only barely afford a near-derelict Austin born the same year as he. He had to rub the tires along curbs to stop. Characteristically, he later claimed this lethal contraption gave him a leg up on his future career:

"The chief qualities of a racing driver are concentration, determination and anticipation. A 1929 Austin without brakes develops all three . . .."

Hill became a racing driver the day he responded to a magazine ad and ponied up a precious pound for four laps in a school car at Brands Hatch. He promptly proposed trading his services as a mechanic for more time on track. Eventually Graham's gamble paid off with some modest racing success, and he began falling in with the right people.

One day after a race he asked for a lift back to London with Lotus men Colin Chapman and Mike Costin. Each assumed he was a friend of the other, which wasn't true, but during the ride the forward young man applied for a job at up-and-coming Lotus. Again it took time and determination, but by 1958 Graham Hill was an F1 driver. It was just five years after he learned to drive a road car.

The first time I remember watching him was on Boxing Day, December 26, 1961, at Brands Hatch. It was a bitterly cold but brilliant day indelibly stamped for me and thousands of others by the red shriek of a V-12 Ferrari sports racing car. In *Autosport* a few days later Hill told us he intentionally kept the revs at redline, rather than changing up, "so the people could hear the lovely noise." How we hailed him for it.

Another favorite Hill memory also involves a Ferrari, this time at Sebring in 1964. By now he was a world champion, and really worth watching, throwing the beast around with the effortless-looking car control that came to him only through endless, dogged practice.

Yanks grew used to seeing this masterful Brit winning our national GP at Watkins Glen, winning so often that we nicknamed the climbing swerves above the pits "Graham Hill." In Monaco he was even more dominant, scoring an unprecedented five victories. (It took 24 years and Ayrton Senna to beat that.)

In my own visits to the Principality, strolling the festive streets the night before the GP, I'd sometimes spot Graham walking to or from the annual gala at the palace, his evening dress immaculate, his erect posture just as they'd taught him in the Royal Navy. You'd think he was the prince of the place.

Some of his countrymen began turning on him in later years. His last Monaco win in 1969 was his last in F1, and as his placings dropped in later seasons, the column-inches began filling with easy potshots: Old Graham's past it, you know, he really ought to step aside, doesn't know when to quit . . ..

For my part, I disdained this crabby tone. The man was a lot faster than I would have been, and he was qualifying, wasn't he? He had paid his dues. Let him enjoy his hard-won skill and keep on living the life we all longed to live.

When he did give up driving, mid-season 1975, he continued as owner of his own F1 team. His elegant red-and-white cars did grace the scene, and he was giving young talent the opportunities he'd been given years before. Who knows what the marque created by this one-time lowly race school mechanic could have achieved?

Sadly, the adventure came to a savage end on the murky night of November 29, 1975. Graham was at the controls of the Piper Aztec that he'd bought with his Indy winnings when it plowed into trees on a golf course a few miles short of his destination in England. Killed with him were his highly promising young driver, Tony Brise, and four other key members of the team.

The tragedy brought out ugliness. In truth, the public hero had been a flawed man in certain ways—yes, I'd seen some—and that got raked up now. A fellow journo seemed excessively pleased to inform me of an irregularity that had come to light involving offshore banking.

I read the official aircraft accident report, which said Hill had neglected to set his altimeter properly, so he was flying lower in the fog than he believed. As he was coming from a day of testing at Paul Ricard in the far south of France, I presume fatigue was a factor, but that's not an excuse.

Hardest of all to forgive, his aircraft licensing and insurance weren't in order, so the bereft families of his team had no recourse but to sue his estate. His widow and children lost everything.

Looking for any brightness, I find it a strangely heartwarming irony that Damon Hill had to launch his racing career from much the same economic level as did his father, which made his own 1993 title all the more meaningful. Damon is still the only second-generation F1 champion.

What I prefer to remember about Graham Hill happened not long before he retired. We were by no means cronies, but I found myself invited to an evening at his very fine, Georgian-style house on the outskirts of London. I couldn't resist exploring, and I was alone in a grand drawing room when my host found me.

I uttered the requisite compliments, he murmured the requisite, "I have to keep pinching m'self, really," and then he startled me by looking shyly down at the polished floor and saying quietly, "I want to thank you for not rubbishing me." In my race reports, he meant.

My heart went out to him. And that's where I'll leave it.

"Heroes are Human Too" won the Motor Press Guild's 2006 Dean Batchelor Award in the category of Best Article of the Year.

10

Phil Hill:
Remembering a Champion

Vintage Racecar, November 2008

THERE WAS THE TIME I went to the Targa Florio and was strolling by a restaurant in the night-dark streets of Palermo just as the reigning world champion popped out. My companion, brasher than I, blurted, "Hey, Phil, can we talk to you?"

"Ya," replied the reigning world champion, and he stopped in his headlong rush and stood there with us, talking. He told us about the 44-mile mountain road circuit and the Ferrari sports racer and how his throttle had stuck and he went over the edge into "a bean field," as I remember he called it.

The reigning world F1 freakin' champion chatting amiably with two utter strangers, just fans, on a spring evening on a sidewalk in Sicily.

This was the first time I'd spoken to him, but not the first time I'd seen him in person. That happened probably two years earlier at Sebring. Midway through a hot Florida afternoon he finished a driving stint, climbed out drenched in sweat and went to a corner of the pit stall, where he slumped to the ground, back against cinder blocks, and lifted a big glass jug of orange juice.

At that instant a man with a microphone bustled in, thrust it out and asked one of those dumb man-with-a-microphone questions.

I was close enough to see Phil's eye measure him up and down. Then he tilted his head back and drained the jug, drained it in one long, throat-pulsing swallow, taking his sweet time, draining it of every

delicious, restorative orange drop. Finally he wiped his sweaty face with the sleeve of his pale blue driving suit. Then, only then, did he began his response to the question.

First things first. I admired Phil Hill for that, and for many other things. No nonsense. No pretense. A straightforward man who raced because he was a racer, just that, and thereby kept the whole thing straight in my mind.

Straightforward, but not simple. Others knew him better than I and have written eloquently about his complexity, but I was able at least to experience some of his independence of thought. One time, long after his racing days, my wife and I went to interview him at Hill and Vaughn, his highly regarded classic car restoration shop.

Leaning back in his classic old desk chair, trying to look at ease but fidgeting continually, swinging back and forth, waving his arms, talking a torrent, he told us many things, but one stands out now in my mind.

Kids today, he said with consternation, are so darn safety-minded. Why, when he takes young people for a ride in some wonderful old car, they look around and complain there aren't any seat belts! He was genuinely puzzled.

I understood perfectly. I watched this man racing when racing was not all about depending on technology for survival, but yourself. Yes, drivers worried about injury and death—so did we passionate onlookers—but the defense measure was to race with intelligence and vigilance and care. Just like flying and motorcycling and shooting, other activities I enjoy precisely because the self-reliance factor is so high.

On another occasion, Phil went on a press trip to Mexico and he brought a knife. A group of us journos were walking along with him through a crowded city street when conversation turned to his record-breaking speed on a particular leg of the old *Carrera Panamericana*. He stopped, unzipped a bag and pulled out the prize he'd been given for that: a *huge* Bowie knife. Unsheathed, it glinted wickedly in the sunlight. Proudly, he showed us the engraved inscription.

I couldn't help but imagine his trying to explain self-reliance and personal responsibility and treasured history to some airline baggage checker who happened to find such a weapon.

Later on that trip each of us got to ride along with Phil along sections of the old *Carrera* route. Honestly, it was hard to relate. The car he was driving was very modern, very high-tech, very smooth and quiet and its road manners were unflawed. Nor was he driving very hard, just a pleasant touring pace. I kept trying to strip away all the luxury and weight and safety measures from my mind, trying to imagine what it had been like to drive these relentlessly rugged roads at racing speed in the sketchy, brutal beasts of half a century before.

I couldn't. The only point at which I caught glimpses was at corner entries. Phil would wait until the *last meter* before he nailed the brakes. That must have been ancient sense-memory I was witnessing. I hoped so.

Everyone who remembers Phil Hill mentions what a fine person he was. A time I saw that side of him was after I'd asked his help with a book about Chaparrals, and had thanked him in the forward. Fully a year after publication I was in Monaco for the GP, and came across Phil also watching the action. Over the screams of engines he made a particular point of expressing his appreciation for mentioning him.

I thought, it isn't often in this business that you get sincere thanks from a racing driver. Mostly, their self-absorbed minds just don't work that way.

And then there was the last time I saw him, at a gala awards function in Los Angeles earlier this year. Phil arrived in a wheelchair, his frailty a shock to anyone who remembered the vigorous athlete he'd been all his life.

He couldn't speak loudly enough to be heard over the noise of the party, but his eyes were still sharp and alert. He was wholly aware of his situation. At one point, as his loyal friend John Lamm wheeled him by where I was, Phil's glance met mine. He smiled, and his eyebrows went up and the look on his face was young and bright. What I believe his expression was saying is, "Isn't this the darndest thing!"

It was work for him to be there, but he came. It was work to stand when acknowledged from the stage, but he stood. It was extremely hard, slow, labored work to sign autographs, but he did it, resolutely, painstakingly, completely. People wanted it, so he obliged.

A gentleman as well as a champion.

This column was one element of a Vintage Racecar *issue paying special tribute to the 2008 passing of America's first World Champion.*

Denny Hulme:
The Bear

Vintage Racecar, January 2006

DRIVERS TODAY TRY to be nice and personable and PR-presentable, even though for some you can tell it's hard work. But there was a time in racing when such individuals figured driving hard was all the work their jobs called for.

"I didn't really enjoy the press a helluva lot . . . I was much happier around the swimming pool at the hotel, and then straight to the circuit and do my thing. Not that I was hiding from the fans or anything like that, but I just wanted to be myself."

That's an F1 World Champion talking. Yes, even with an attitude like that, which earned him the nickname "The Bear," Denis Clive Hulme reached the top of his profession. He was especially successful in America, where marketability is All, being a contender at Indianapolis as well as by far the most accomplished driver in the "Million-Dollar Can-Am."

The Bear managed all that without once suffering a fool. "What I found in America," he'd growl, "is that everybody wants to come up and tell you how you should be running your car, or what it's doing around the circuit. But, Christ, I was driving the thing. I knew. I had enough problems without everybody telling me what the problems were."

The Bear once found a careless mechanic had left a roll of racer-tape in his cockpit. You know the heft of one of those. Visualize a big orange McLaren Can-Am car blasting by the pit wall at full bellow and out of it bulleting an object hurled with the full force of a burly, angry arm. I believe the hapless crewman survived.

The Bear would eye new "bits" with no attempt to disguise wary skepticism. A McLaren fabricator told me about one day proudly showing Denny an elaborate new throttle mechanism he'd worked up, guaranteed to operate smoothly and without jamming. "The bloke picked it up and just *twisted* it in those big 'ands of 'is, and the bloody thing bent like a *pretzel*. I mean he *knackered* it. He gave it back and said, 'Make it stronger,' and walked off."

When I repeated that to Denny, years later, he burst into that endearing, tongue-out giggle of his. "Well, it was never any fun going to the circuit and thinking, 'Geesh, this is going to snap.' I'd go and sit in a car and put all the weight I could on a brake pedal or something to see if I could break it or bend it."

There's another story that The Bear once ripped a gearshifter out by its roots. His physique was built in his youth in New Zealand, where he'd worked for his dad's construction company, shoveling a lot of sand into a lot of trucks. McLaren race cars of his day were known for their sturdiness, and I have no doubt Denny Hulme is a big reason why.

But the man was way more than muscle. Get past the brusque, defensive exterior—it was possible, if you were sensible and not pushy— and you'd find a soul of warmth and a mind of keen intelligence. Denny was more a listener than a talker, but when he did say something it sounded right. He had the calm eye of a self-made person, one able and accustomed to solving problems with his own hands. Always interested in the mechanisms of things, he liked to watch his crew working on his cars. Often he'd pick up a spanner to help.

I can't say how the mechanics felt about that, but I do know his team's inner circle remember him with fondness and gratitude. They say that when Bruce McLaren was killed, Hulme was the tower of leadership who kept them together and going forward.

That was despite searing agony in both hands caused by a fuel fire at Indianapolis. He turned up for the next race regardless, driving with his paws swathed in bandages, charred skin peeling off inside and blood soaking the gauze. He led many laps of that race.

And how he could drive! Hulme didn't always seem inspired, in fact he sometimes looked positively lazy, but when his blood got up his driving could make your jaw drop. He appeared to lift a car up by sheer brute force and hurl it around the course, his work at the wheel looking like, OK, like a bear trashing a cabin.

Yet no matter how heavy you thought his hands were on the car, he understood it and was not hurting it. And despite the seeming fury of his mood, part of his mind was sitting back, thinking.

I witnessed this from his passenger seat. One of my best-ever weekends in motorsport was spent as Denny's navigator on a three-day celebrity rally called the Tour of Britain. He'd never driven a rally before (or so he claimed) and it was fascinating to watch him learn about it. The Bear would sniff out a new situation cautiously, taking it in, thinking it over, and only then would his foot go down. Hard. Hanging on alongside, I watched him do screaming-sideways things with an automobile I hadn't known were possible.

On the last morning of that rally, we were flailing through a Special Stage, gravel flying, when he announced in a shout, "I'm losin' the gearbox, Pete!" Oh, rats, I thought, we've come all this way and now we're out.

No, we weren't. With growing incredulity, I watched my burly Bear tenderly nurse that transmission on through the rest of the day. Absolutely nothing else went out of his driving, he was still a tornado on the other controls, but every time he reached for the shifter he . . . just . . . gentled . . . it. I'd already realized I could never drive as fast as he; now I witnessed a mental discipline I can only admire from afar. We did make it to the finish, winning our class and placing sixth overall.

At the time he retired from F1, at the end of 1973, World Champ Denny Hulme ranked as the sixth-best driver in Grand Prix history.

He's still Best Bear in my book.

12

James Hunt:
Britain's Shooting Star

Vintage Racecar, February 2003

HIS TEAM OWNER called him "Superstar." It was fitting. Some who liked him less called him "Shunt." That too was apt. When James Hunt first burst onto the F1 scene in 1973, he was thought a bit of a joke, a talented but impetuous n'er-do-well from the lesser ranks who was always going on his 'ead.

Three years later he was World Champion.

Tall, blond, memorably good looking in a rawboned way, bright, articulate, famous, and, at last, rich, James seemed born to the playboy lifestyle, and he lived it flat-out. You could make a movie about his love affairs. But you made a grievous mistake if you saw no more in the man.

Alexander Hesketh was even richer, and a baron besides; he could live any way he pleased, and did. It was his Lordship's pleasure to create his own Formula 1 racing team (in an era when that still was possible for private individuals). He chose to fund it on his own, disdaining sponsorship, and he made the grandest possible Grand Prix entrance, joining the Circus for the first time at Monte Carlo. The team had a yacht stationed in the harbor, which was *de rigueur*, and also a helicopter perched on the quai, which was singular. Alexander flew it himself. He was 23.

Hesketh's team manager was known as Bubbles. Their car designer was called Doc. Others were String, Ferret, and Thomas the Tank Engine. Their mascot was a teddy bear, images of which adorned everything from T-shirts (highly popular!) to the otherwise sober grey walls of the Hesketh estate, which housed the race shop.

You had only to walk by Hesketh's corner of the paddock to see how much fun these guys were having. But if you saw no more, you were blind. Whatever the outside world thought, the team wasn't there for the fun. Every man jack thought only about winning. They never stopped thinking about how to accomplish it.

I came to appreciate the secretly cerebral side of this flamboyant group because one season I was asked to write a small book about James, and that meant talking to key figures in greater depth than is typically required for race reports.

Here's some of what Team Manager Anthony "Bubbles" Horsley, himself a former race driver, said about their Superstar:

"James (pause) . . . is greedy (another pause) . . . is basically interested in James Hunt, so he has a large ego. . . He has a boyish charm, so one finds it difficult to say no to him. He's very intelligent, which is possibly a mixed blessing . . . .

His Lordship with Superstar at the Hesketh estate, 1975.

"We did know he was good, but we're beginning to think he may be something special."

Engineer and car designer Harvey Postlethwaite, aka "Doc," assessed James this way: "He's of the thinking school of Grand Prix drivers, like Fittipaldi and like Lauda. Based on his experience he can discern between Black Art and technology . . ..

"He always knows what's happening with the car, in detail, and he automatically ties the important facts together. That's his real strength as a driver."

James told me this about himself: "I don't consider myself as somebody who's got enormous natural talent. I put myself in the second rank, behind Peterson . . .. Maybe I can't do one-off, banzai laps in practice like Ronnie, but I reckon I can get the job done over 80 laps."

A friend who sat down with James for a game of backgammon found herself locked into it for hours. "Whew. He never lets you off the hook!"

His business manager, Barrie Gill, told me he thought James wasn't so much a race driver as a highly competitive sportsman who happened to find his outlet in a car. James endorsed that when he remarked that he was 17 before he ever had any thought of racing.

"As a boy I was only really interested in sports. I was mainly motivated by competition . . .. I was keen on tennis and squash.

"I had learnt to drive only the year before and I'm afraid I was a bit of a terror on the public road; it was that competition thing again. Well, one day I went along to a motor race meeting with some of my mates, and that was it, it was instant commitment.

"You see, I'd never known there was such a thing as club racing. So far as I knew motor racing was something impossibly remote, a thing carried out by Jim Clark and a lot of Continentals with long names. I couldn't identify with them at all. But *here* suddenly was something within reach of a mere mortal."

Hunt first raced his own Mini, then moved through Formula Ford to F3, and in 1971 March took him on as a works driver. But a year later the factory dropped him. Too many wrecks. "Hunt the Shunt" looked to be at the end of his brief career.

That's when Hesketh and Horsley picked him up for their own struggling small-bore operation.

"We sort of found each other," Bubbles explained. "We sort of needed each other. Nobody was exactly knocking on our door, we were frankly a huge bloody joke as an F3 team. Nobody was about to give him a drive, either.

"But he looked right. You looked at him and you said to yourself, 'Now that bloke ought to be quick.' You couldn't put your finger on it, it was just a feeling."

Instant turnaround? Hardly. There were promising moments, but disappointing results. By the spring of 1973, Hesketh Racing was at the point where an average team would have given up.

It was the point Alexander said, "Let's have a crack at the real thing."

He bought an F1 March and entered James in the Monaco Grand Prix. James was 25. It really was his last chance. If this were a screenplay, we'd have the kid winning first time out. Reality was almost as unbelievable: after qualifying 18th out of 26, not at all bad for a first-timer, Hunt moved up to sixth place in the race—only to have the engine blow three laps from the end.

In his second GP, the French, he did finish sixth to score his first-ever championship point. Race three was home at Silverstone, where James placed fourth. Next time, in Holland, he came third! Why, at this rate . . ..

No, he never did score a win that year, but he did finish a close, storming second to Peterson at the USGP, and wound up eighth in the championship after running but eight of the season's 15 GPs.

The next year Postlethwaite designed a Hesketh car, and in 1975 James drove it to victory in the Dutch GP.

I wish this *were* a movie. I'd script it so gallant little Hesketh Racing would build on that success and win the championship with their Superstar. They certainly had the talent.

But not the resources. In the third season even His Lordship had to start looking for sponsorship; when he couldn't secure enough, his team folded. James Hunt, now a proven professional, thanks to Hesketh, went straight to McLaren, promptly won six more GPs in 1976 and, in that year's dramatic, rain-soaked race in Japan he seized the world driving title for England. That's how the Brits I was with that night looked at it. They wouldn't stop singing, "We are the Champions . . .."

Unfortunately, real life moved on past the happy ending. James became less and less of a factor, and it must have been frustration that brought back his early rep as a wild child both on and off the track. After a dismal 1979 season he stepped out of the cockpit, though not out of the public eye; he proved a big hit as a TV racing commentator.

I'd be happy to write that as the end of the bright story. Sadly, Britain's Superstar died of a heart attack in 1993. He was only 45.

Yet, as movies teach us, the ending is only one part. Look back at the significance of what James Hunt achieved. That's the real story.

13

Oscar Koveleski

Vintage Racecar, July 2008

OSCAR KOVELESKI CALLED the other day, and when our talk was done I felt like I always do: as if I'd just been inside a dyno cell with a red-hot race engine at fever pitch. The man must be a decade richer in experiences than I, yet I'm left panting by his everlasting enthusiasm, energy and endurance.

Had I ever been a Can-Am driver, as Oscar was, I imagine I'd have felt like that every time Denny Hulme blew by.

It's thanks to the Can-Am that I met Oscar, and the grand old series keeps bringing us back together. At one reunion I was supposed to step up to a lectern and say something. Sensing my panic, Oscar offered kind advice: keep it short and simple. I did, and the ordeal was over before I knew it.

Not that he follows that principle himself. Koveleski calls are always entertaining and enlightening, but tend to be lengthy and mono-directional. Oscar seldom closes a sentence, as his supercharged mind keeps packing one new idea, memory, comment, question, quote or joke on top of another in a breathless stream of incandescent consciousness. I imagine listening to this prepares one for standing in the middle of the grid as the flag drops.

He might start musing about reviving the Can-Am, say, then shift to driving advice Mark Donohue once gave him, veer to international trade, drift toward military history, carom into the state of motorsports today, brush the guardrail of national politics, downshift to a story of racing Jackie Stewart at slot cars, chicane neatly into the latest news about his own beloved Kidracers (child-sized electric cars) and powerslide out with one of his favorite quotes:

"If everybody's thinkin' the same, nobody's thinking. Know who said that? General! George! Patton!"

It was Oscar's inventive brain that came up with a way to enliven Can-Am lunch breaks: mechanics' creeper races. He also established the Pole Position Pole, an actual metal stave awarded for . . . well, I never quite grasped the rules.

Of course Oscar Koveleski will live forever as president of the Polish Racing Drivers Association, founded in 1970 with two fellow fun-lovers, driver Tony Adamowicz and PR man Brad Niemcek. The PRDA's rules I did get. You were eligible to join if you were a Polish racing driver, a non-Polish racing driver, a Polish non-racing driver, or a non-Polish non-racing driver.

Koveleski, in hat, with crew chief Jack Deren and driver Tony Adamowicz, McLaren M8B, at Watkins Glen, 1971.

I was pleased to find I qualified, and Oscar tells me I am member number 54. Everybody is—just like his race cars. Yes, that's in honor of the old "Car 54" TV show.

One time an official PRDA manila envelope arrived. Inside I found a single sheet of entirely blank paper. I still count this among the most informative press releases I've ever received.

In 1971, Brad, Tony and Oscar competed in Brock Yates' inaugural Cannonball Baker Sea to Shining Sea Memorial Trophy Dash. While Yates himself cadged a Ferrari Daytona and talked Dan Gurney into driving it, the PRDA entry was a Chevy van stuffed full of gasoline barrels and a bunk bed in a bid to go non-stop from New York to California. It might have worked but for a fuel system glitch that cost time. The Chevy van finished second to the 172-mph Ferrari by a scant 53 minutes.

After years of SCCA club racing (MG TC, Chevy-engined Ferrari), Oscar came into the Can-Am in 1969 with a McLaren M6B. He was an instant breath of fresh air. That was the year the McLaren factory team won all 11 races in their winged M8Bs, so to match their technology Oscar fitted an airfoil just like theirs ... but on his helmet, not his car.

At the end of the season he bought Bruce McLaren's championship-winning M8B and campaigned it through the next two years, scoring a career-high fourth place at Road Atlanta in 1970. At the same track the same car took Koveleski to an SCCA National Championship.

Partway through Can-Am 1971 he stepped out in favor of Adamowicz, who immediately started qualifying the two-year-old chassis seventh and eighth on the grids and finishing as high as third (Mid-Ohio). Though Tony "A-to-Z" only ran 6 of that year's 10 races, he placed seventh in points.

The Clown Prince of the Can-Am; I've called Oscar that, but the fun he was making had a purpose. As a cast member of the Bruce and Denny Show, the businessman in him well understood the bad rap the McLaren-dominated series was getting for being too predictable. Boring, some called it. Oscar took it as his mission to liven things up.

In this PC world it's only among fellow racers that he could get away with this one: hauling me and designer Peter Bryant together with himself, his arms clamped over our shoulders, and yelling, "Hey, look—a Polak with two peters!"

I've even fallen victim to a pure-Oscar joke on the highway. As I overtook his motorhome, he turned his head and grinned *with vampire fangs!* Imagine the effect on motorists who didn't recognize him.

Oscar credits his wife, Elaine, and Terry Deren, wife of crew chief Jack, for the best Can-Am gag I know of. Cleaning out a tin of Johnson Wax, the orange goop made by the series sponsor, she refilled it with butterscotch pudding and conspired to be eating it just as the head of the company walked by.

Oscar is a promoter by birth. When he brought his father to a race it was like being with twins. Anthony Koveleski is well remembered in the hobby world for his miniature cars and model kits, so in 1958 it was natural for Oscar to open a mail order business he called Auto World. He also started a magazine on car modeling. Later he organized and promoted SCCA races at Pocono, and recently he and Jack Deren released their own Can-Am DVD.

Oscar inaugurated Kidracers in 1988 with an event at Watkins Glen. Since then he reckons he has introduced "probably 50,000 or 100,000" children ages 3 to 7 to driving and to racing. What a great project (see kidracers.com).

See what I mean about inexhaustible energy?

Oscar often signs off a phone call with, "You're my buddy an' I love ya." I know he says that to everybody, but I do feel the same.

14

Bruce McLaren's Legacy

Vintage Racecar, September 2007

BRUCE LESLIE MCLAREN won the first-ever Grand Prix of the United States in 1959, but really established his life's legacy eight years later. It was September 3, 1967, at Road America when his Can-Am team began a five-year run of dominance in the fastest kind of road racing the world had ever seen.

So strong and so solid was the foundation laid then that McLaren remains one of the greatest names in motorsports today.

Kiwis can be crusty—they're not alone in this—but Bruce was blessed with one of the sunniest natures ever to venture north from New Zealand. Open of face, friendly of manner, self-effacing and always on the brink of a laugh, he had a gift for bringing talented and ambitious racers—not the easiest of personality types—together in a loyal, tight-knit, intensely competitive team.

McLaren also stood out for blending exceptional driving ability with his education in engineering. He was always bubbling with ideas to improve his cars, which he would then personally evaluate at speed. Yet, entirely typical of the man, he would grinningly discount himself in both areas. Bruce showed no reluctance to hire drivers even faster than he was, and when discussing new concepts with his designers and fabricators he'd say, "Make it simple enough even I can understand it!"

The simple, sturdy, eminently pragmatic racing cars his company turned out reflected Bruce's own straightforward approach to life.

Born in August 1937, the son of an Auckland garage owner, McLaren started competing with his own small Austin car at 16. By 20 he was driving Cooper racing cars, and in 1958 won his enthusiastic nation's annual driver-to-Europe scholarship program. Cooper gave him a Formula 2 ride, and he did so well that in 1959 they moved him up to F1 to partner Jack Brabham.

That was Black Jack's first championship season, of course, but at the British GP young Bruce set fastest lap and finished third. Then, at Sebring in the inaugural U.S. Grand Prix right at the end of the year, McLaren was holding second when Brabham ran out of gas. Presto, the 22-year-old rookie was a winner.

That early success in America seems to have set a path for McLaren, as he went on to be a major player in professional sports car racing in both the U.S. and Canada. While still at Cooper, on the side he became a constructor in his own right. With a small group of buddies, including Americans Tyler Alexander and Teddy Mayer, he further modified a former Cooper F1 chassis that Roger Penske had turned into a sports racer (the "Zerex Special") by installing Oldsmobile's aluminum V-8.

Dubbed the "Jolly Green Giant," this unabashed hot rod promptly won its first race at Mosport in 1964, Bruce beating the likes of Jim Hall in a Chaparral and A.J. Foyt in a Scarab.

That fall McLaren finished his first all-McLaren sports car, the M1A. This and successors earned good money in North America and elsewhere through early 1966, but when the big-bucks Canadian-American Challenge Cup series launched in September of that year, Bruce felt personally humiliated to find himself left behind by Chaparral and Lola.

Determined to step up its program for 1967, McLaren's team designed an all-new car, the M6. It featured a stiff monocoque chassis rather than the tube frames used earlier, a high-downforce body reflecting Bruce's experience with the Ford GT40 program (he

co-drove to a Le Mans win in 1966), and stout small-block Chevy engines featuring fuel injection, then a novelty, tuned by another American, Gary Knutson.

But McLaren knew design is one thing, development another; aided by BRM running late on the engines he wanted to use in F1, Bruce spent months fine-tuning his sports car. As his new teammate, fellow Kiwi Denny Hulme, later commented, "We got those cars perfect, so when we came racing, we were ready to go racing. We weren't ready to go testing."

Turned out in a bold caramel color, the two McLarens sparkled at the head of the long Road America grid. Bruce won pole with a lap *10 seconds better* than any previous time there. An oil leak stopped him in the race, but Denny effortlessly took over, winning at an average race speed higher than the previous single-lap record.

So began the Can-Am's "Bruce and Denny Show." The Kiwis went on to win five of that year's six races, and McLaren himself became the 1967 series Champion. Hulme took the title the next year and McLaren repeated in 1969—a year with 11 races, of which Bruce or Denny won every one.

Ten days before the 1970 Can-Am was to start, Bruce McLaren died in a testing accident. The tragedy only seemed to toughen his team, with Bruce's good friend Dan Gurney stepping in to win the first two races and Hulme finishing the year with another championship. In 1971 another American, Peter Revson, earned McLaren's fifth title in a row.

The strong little team Bruce built managed two more victories in 1972 against the well-funded might of Penske's turbocharged Porsches. Then Teddy Mayer had to face financial reality and pull out of the Can-Am. But if you know your F1 and Indy car history, you know the rest of the Bruce McLaren legacy. It's one of the brightest in all of auto racing.

15

Ronnie Peterson

Vintage Racecar, March 2010

WE SPRANG OVER the crest of Paddock Hill Bend at 80 mph or more, the little Lotus Europa cocked way sideways, scrawny tires screaming. I was trying to burrow into the passenger side of the cockpit, jamming my knees against the insides of the legwell, both hands gripping . . . whatever they could grip. I wasn't scared, not exactly, but I was very, very alert.

Think of the word tense. Well, Ronnie Peterson was the opposite of that. A tranquil fellow at any time, in this circumstance he appeared nearly torpid, his tall frame slouched low in the seat, one long forearm resting on the center console, pale, slender fingers lightly massaging the gear lever.

The only part of him moving fast was his other hand, the one whipping the Lotus's little leather steering wheel back and forth, three to nine, three to nine, chasing the wobbly waggles provoked by the bumpy old Brands Hatch surface.

There we were, heeled over, clocking 80-plus, catching slides . . . and my driver was hardly paying attention. He certainly wasn't looking where we were going.

Out of the corners of my own widened eyes I could see that, all the while we were howling up and over and down the far side of Brands's infamously dramatic first turn, opposite-locking all the way, Ronnie

Petersen kept his placid Nordic face swiveled toward me.

He was talking to me. Anything to occupy his mind.

It is truly said that the most gifted of racing drivers operate on a different plane, but the statement carries no meaning until you experience it happening with your own life hanging in their hands.

That moment measured the gulf between us, and between ordinary cars and Grand Prix machinery. I was as close to my own limit as that little mid-engined Europa street car was to its. Ronnie was . . . bored.

Liquid natural speed like a plunging mountain torrent; that's what Ronnie Peterson looked like in a racing car.

He first surged into my awareness in 1971, during the streaming wet Canadian GP at Mosport. I'd seen him race a couple of times before, but results had been lackluster, and until now I hadn't personally witnessed why everyone in F1 was talking about "Super Swede."

He was driving a "Tea Trey" March 711 that year, the model whose nickname deriving from its Spitfire-like ovoid front wing perched on a pylon atop the rounded nose. During Saturday practice March designer Robin Herd remarked that, although they'd just fixed a broken front roll bar, "He never complains if there's too much *oversteer*."

My interest piqued, I tramped out to the embankment high outside Mosport's dropping Turn 1 and began scribbling notes for the report I would write Sunday night for *Autosport*.

"Ronnie was not complaining," I reported. "He was getting the 711 right up on the edge, and overstepping the edge with a very smooth, delicate, calm touch . . . ."

"His hurling of the March down through the first turn was splendid to watch, the car often getting well sideways both before and after the power went on, but Ronnie himself never seemed in any kind of hurry. His control of a slide was almost languid, and was never overdone. He almost seemed to be saying, 'Oh, if you want me to catch you I suppose I really must, but it's such a bother.'"

Segment timing with my windup-style stopwatch showed he was getting through the turn as fast as anybody and faster than most. Around the lap as a whole, the official watches ranked him fifth.

That was in the dry. Sunday's race was slithery wet. Petersen made a beautifully aggressive start, squeezing between other cars and the pit wall and by Turn 2 he was second. That put him right on the tail of poleman Jackie Stewart's Tyrrell.

It was pouring rain, a cold Canadian September rain that drenched the track and the grass and the mud and all of us watching, but did not damp what we were watching.

"They were all traveling at walking pace, on tiptoes," I wrote, "the cars sliding right across the full width of the road and swerving viciously at any hint of throttle. The spume from the naked tyres, hurled aloft by the airfoils, was blinding."

Watching in a state of enchantment, I saw Jackie Stewart, who had just clinched his second World Championship and was showing us why, begin to pull away in the clear. But then Ronnie Peterson, young sensation, showed me why his name was on everyone's lips. He was the first man I saw try something different. He started running wide in the turns, finding a rougher surface strewn with grit that gave him more grip. Dramatically, he began closing on Stewart. I wrote about it:

"The Scot, who must have had time to decide he already had the race won, suddenly noticed that troublesome March front wing in his mirrors again. After the race, said Ronnie, 'He admit to me that I learn him the right line to take.'

"It was now a race between Stewart and Peterson, nose to tail, wheel to wheel, Goodyear to Firestone. Four times around the back Ronnie scrambled by Jackie, once on the outside of Turn 2, three times on either the inside or outside of Turn 3. Three times the World Champion got it back before the end of the lap, once because the March got off on to mud, once because the Scot 'snookered' the Swede onto an inferior piece of track with a slower car they were lapping, and once on slipstreaming at the top of the long straight . . . .

"All the time they were right together, splashing over the glistening surface, breathing each other's spray, both ends of both cars breaking loose with little sideways slithers, both engines suddenly winding up towards redline in uncontrolled bursts in the puddles. . ."

One time that Peterson got ahead he stayed ahead for 13 gleeful laps. But then, on a lap when Stewart had retaken the point again, the blue Tyrrell managed to scramble by a backmarker but the red March didn't. Nose touched wheel and Ronnie spun.

He gathered it up and continued, still in second place, but he'd lost time and now his "tea tray" was askew and one front brake was locking. Our great Grand Prix was over. But it lives on in my memory as one of the best.

In subsequent seasons I was privileged to see Ronnie Peterson's magic again and again. I'll never forget his incredible save of a Lotus 72 in Argentina 1973, his first race with the car, when it snapped sideways, literally sideways, and I had scarcely started to think "it's gone" when

Ronnie snapped it back straight, dead straight, no fishtailing at all, nor any letup at all in the blue haze coming off his fat back tires.

Or the way he came shooting into the ultra-fast old Woodcote corner at Silverstone, pitching the little black wedge into oversteer and holding it there, holding opposite lock and full throttle all the way through, going so fast it was hard to swing your eyes to keep up.

I imagine he wasn't bored then.

16

Our Brian Redman

Vintage Racecar, September 2003

THE BRIT WHO Conquered the Colonies; I know that title's not fair to others of his countrymen who also have raced brilliantly in America, but sorry, chaps, it's how I think of Brian Redman.

We Yanks just love the bloke.

Why? It's an exceptional blend of several things, I think. Certainly one is his success during his professional career. Driving Formula 1, and Formula 5000 open-wheelers, and also Can-Am, FIA and IMSA sports cars and coupes, this lad from Lancashire has raced internationally with such factory teams as Aston Martin, BMW, BRM, Chevron, Cooper, Ferrari, Ford, Jaguar, Lola, McLaren, Porsche, and Shadow.

He helped some of those manufacturers win championships: in 1968 (John Wyer Ford), 1969 (Porsche), 1970 (Chevron and Porsche) and 1972 (Ferrari). In the US, he was champion of SCCA F5000 in 1974, 1975 and 1976 (Lola T330 and T332), and added the IMSA GTP title in 1981 (Chevy-Lola T600).

The Redman race record is too long to list here, but it includes victories in such major long-distance events as the Brands Hatch 6-Hours (two wins), Daytona 24-Hr. (three), Kyalami 9-Hr. (two), Monza 1000-Kilometers (two), Nurburgring 1000K (two), Sebring 12-Hr. (two), Spa 1000K, and the epic Targa Florio.

Beyond his talent with big, powerful race cars, Brian was notable for his careful intelligence at the wheel. Stories abound of his seemingly prescient ability to avoid trouble in circumstances that had others crashing left and right. Driving an awesome Porsche 917 at the infamously fast Spa, for instance, he once came up to a blind turn and—for some reason—backed off early. It was just early enough to avoid the wreckage from another driver's accident.

The clue? He hadn't seen any yellow flags, he told journalist Denis Jenkinson. But he had noticed, subliminally, something different about the spectators. On every previous lap, their faces were turned to him. This time he was seeing backs of heads.

I was at the same circuit another time, when Brian was driving a Ferrari 312P, and he noticed his friends behind the fences bustling to don jackets and put up umbrellas. It was enough warning to let him slither safely through a sudden rain squall that was wetting the far side of the turn.

A moment later, one of his teammates came rushing into the same corner at full speed, and—CLANG!

At Road America during one of his F5000 drives, he lifted off the gas just *before* the Lola's rear suspension broke. He told me he'd seen the link in his mirror as it started to give way. "Brian," I said thoughtfully, "knowing you, I wouldn't be surprised to learn you deliberately set your mirrors to keep an eye on your rear suspension."

He tried to look modest. "Well, yes, actually, I do."

So speak with Brian Redman, and you're hearing from of one of the most accomplished and respected figures in motorsport. But that's not all.

When some star drivers retire, they abandon us. Brian has remained intensely active in vintage racing. Not only does he drive—and with "heart and fire," as he puts it—he provides venues for others to drive. His annual Jefferson 500 is known as one of the finer historic meetings in the U.S., while his Targa 66, a limited membership club, is a hit with owners who enjoy exercising their machines in a less competitive environment than racing.

And Brian sure knows how to make it enjoyable. One of the all-time great storytellers, he is an absolute fountain of fun. I've been at the dinner table when his wife, Marion, touched his hand and murmured, "Not so loud, dear." But she was laughing as hard as everyone else.

Is all that enough to win our hearts? Maybe, but to me there's a clincher about the man: his humanity. By that I mean the human emotion he's not shy about showing, and the fact that he hasn't tried to hide the internal struggle I suspect all drivers feel about driving.

Brian actually retired, or tried to, mid-career. It was a dark time in racing, with fatal accidents almost routine. He himself had suffered a terrifying crash at Spa in 1968, when the front suspension of his F1 Cooper broke at 150 mph. At the end of 1970, having scored several good wins, Redman announced his time had come to quit. He moved to South Africa for a settled life in the dealership business.

It wasn't the life for him. He was soon back in a race car, and back in victory circle. And, unfortunately, back in hospital. Early in 1971, at Sicily's wild Targa Florio, his Porsche 908 broke its steering and veered into a cement post. Brian suffered serious burns, especially on his face.

Typically, he makes hilarious light of it today. Because of skin grafts, he told writer Bill Oursler, "When I get a kiss from a nice lady, I have to tell them they're kissing my left buttock!"

That crash was bad enough, but worse came a few years later at St. Jovite in Canada. At a crest in the track the wide-bodied Lola he was driving lifted its nose so high it flipped over backwards, crashing heavily. Then—and again, this is one of the great Brian Redman stories—he rode through a second crash when the ambulance rushing him to hospital blew a tire.

So when you watch him strap into a race car today, you can be sure he knows what he's doing—in every sense. And you understand how much driving means to him.

In my mind, having Brian Redman part of our sport makes it not only important and enjoyable, but also more deeply meaningful. Thank you, Sir Brian.

17

Peter Revson:
Memory of a Warrior

Vintage Racecar, January 2004

THIRTY YEARS AGO the world was no less crassly simplistic than it is today, and many people glancing at Peter Revson only wanted to see his glamorous lifestyle and gorgeous girlfriends; a privileged, pretty boy at play.

What I preferred to see was his marvelous talent, his quiet, thoughtful intelligence, and his determination to fulfill his life's potentials on his own terms.

He was well on the way to that in F1. I remember a conversation at Silverstone early in his second year as a McLaren factory driver. How did he think he was getting along in this ferocious European milieu? "You know," he said, his brow wrinkling in puzzlement over his deep, intense eyes, "everybody raves about how fast Ronnie Peterson is, but I can stay with him, and I think he's kind of ragged and inconsistent. I think I'm smoother than he is."

That exchange took place the day before the 1973 British Grand Prix, the race in which Peter "Rich American" Revson scored his breakthrough first F1 victory—beating pole-starter Ronnie "Super Swede" Peterson.

By the end of that season Revson had won his second GP, the

Revvie with Denny at Mosport, 1971.

Canadian at Mosport. He ranked fifth in the world championship, as he had the year before. I thought then, and believe now, that "Revvie" was on his way to genuine greatness as an American Formula 1 driver.

But no matter how much we wish our racing stories all had happy endings, this one didn't. Only months later Peter Jeffrey Revlon Revson died suddenly, violently, and far too young. He'd only just turned 35.

Such tragedies were almost routine then. During the years I covered GP racing, in that series alone we typically lost one or two drivers a year. In '73, the toll had been Roger Williamson at Zandvoort and Francois Cevert at Watkins Glen. Following Revson's death in March of 1974 at Kyalami, Helmuth Koinigg would be the second in a row killed at the Glen.

I remember feeling, not callous, but cautious. I didn't want to get too close to these guys. But it was hard not to warm to Revvie.

For one thing, I appreciated his wanting to prove himself as an individual. He and younger brother Douglas, also a racer, were indeed born into privilege. Their father had been a co-founder of the Revlon cosmetics empire. A wealthy background can have two edges, but Peter had also inherited an iron independence. When he set out to become a serious racer, he took a hard, honest road.

His first racing was in 1960, with his own Morgan in Hawaii. The story goes that he won his second race, but after his third the local club banned him for being too aggressive! A useful trait for a racing driver, of course, and Revvie was intent on being one. Back at the family seat in New York he bought a Formula Junior. Results were encouraging, and in 1963 Peter ventured to Europe. No idle playboy, he helped his mechanic work on their car and also drove—and slept in—the transporter, an old baker's van nicknamed "Gilbert."

Fun times, and success began coming too. By 1965 he had made the transition from sportsman to pro, when as a paid member of a team supported by the Lotus factory America's Peter Revson won the important Monaco F3 race. A year later, he was asked to race a GT40 internationally, and also started getting Can-Am and Trans-Am rides in the U.S.

Then in 1967 Doug Revson was killed in a racing accident.

During the few years I knew Peter I never asked him about losing his brother. That dread of involvement. Today, I've searched through the book he wrote with Leon Mandel, "Speed with Style," and I see his biographer got no closer on this point. Mandel says Revson didn't talk about it. Leon can only describe Peter going to the funeral and then straight to a Trans-Am in New Hampshire, "where, expressionless, he won the second race in a row for the Cougar racing team."

What I think is that the danger loomed so large that nobody wanted to look it in the eye. Yes, people were aware of the risks and doing their best about them. Incremental improvements were being made. But by today's enormously advanced standards the cars were flimsy, the tracks were festooned with hazards, and safety—and medical—equipment was primitive. A driver determined to continue racing could only resolve to do it as carefully as possible, then close his mind and press on, trusting his ability to keep him alive.

What I also think is that this dare-the-devil self-reliance was part of racing's appeal in those days. I deeply admired such people. I saw them as warriors, maybe even as heroes.

Where I saw most of Revvie at first was in the Can-Am, where he was smooth and quick and an ever-strengthening force until McLaren hired him in 1971. Then he won five races to teammate Denny Hulme's three (and Lola factory driver Jackie Stewart's two) and became the first American Can-Am champ. At the same time he showed standout speed in Indy cars, taking pole and finishing second in the '71 500. The "rich kid from New York," as I heard a track announcer call him, was a real driver.

Revson moved to Shadow for '74—a top American driver joining an American F1 team! Later that year Mario Andretti and Mark Donohue would come in with two more American teams, Vel's Parnelli Jones and Penske. What a different world it was.

Shadow was founded by Don Nichols, a U.S. entrepreneur with international interests. Shadow started competing in the Can-Am in 1970. In 1973, Nichols expanded the team's efforts to include F1.

That first year Shadow's American driver George Follmer scored two points-paying finishes in his rookie F1 season. With double Grand Prix winner Revson aboard a brand-new car for '74, I for one expected Shadow to be very strong.

On the first day of practice for the first GP of the year, in Argentina, Revvie was second-fastest. His time didn't hold up for day two and he started the race from fourth place. Still not bad, but the brand-new car let him down. In Brazil he qualified sixth, but though again the car failed to go the distance he said it was coming along.

The last time I saw him was at a cold and rainy non-championship F1 event at Brands Hatch. Revson wasn't a factor for the lead, but Denny Hulme's column in *Autosport* spoke admiringly of watching his former teammate find a different line through the fast Paddock Bend that let him rush up on opponents into the slow Druids hairpin.

From there Revvie went with the rest of the Circus to sunny South Africa for testing prior to the GP there. I headed with British colleagues to the Le Mans test weekend. En route down through France, we heard the news on the car radio. "American racing driver Peter Revson . . .." The front suspension had broken and the Shadow slammed into steel guardrails, which burst apart and ripped the aluminum chassis to shreds.

Hulme was one of the first on the scene. A long time later he told me that, as he grasped Revson in a bear hug to haul him from the burning wreckage, he could feel Peter's heart still beating. But it was too late.

It was too late way too often in those days.

We always feel a need to find something positive in these tragedies. I keep telling myself that, had he not raced, I'd never have known of this person, never had a chance to enjoy his company, to appreciate his talent, to cheer his battle. For we're all in battles of our own, and we do draw inspiration from our fellow warriors.

18

In Praise of Mechanics

Vintage Racecar, July 2005

As SOMEONE WHOSE own hands have all the finesse of lead knock-off hammers, I've always admired those deft artisans of racing, the gifted mechanics whose fingers appear as instruments of divine grace, crafting beauty with effortless gestures. Besides, they're really the people who make the sport happen.

Schumacher is a terrific driver, sure, but where would he be without a good car under him? Well, so far this year we've seen exactly where—nowhere!

No, drivers and engineers and managers and PR reps and, of course, reporters may all be important, but mechanics are the true foundation stones of motorsport. We fans like to count Henry Ford as a racer, at least in his early days, but he was first of all a mechanic who made his name as a racer and then as an automaker literally by making his cars with his own hands. Most of his fellow pioneers did the same (not to mention those brilliant bicycle mechanics who invented aviation).

Though the auto biz at large has changed, in racing the road to the top can still start in a toolbox.

We think of both Hills—Phil and Graham—as F1 driving champions, but both began their racing careers as mechanics. So did one of Phil's own race mechanics, Richie Ginther, who as a Ferrari factory driver blended both his talents to devise the first aerodynamic spoiler. John Surtees, world champion on bikes and in cars, grew up fettling his own machines. Mark Donohue's hands were on his cars as frequently as anyone's. Can-Am's Great Bear, Denny Hulme, was often seen with a spanner in his paw (between naps). When A.J. Foyt stopped driving he didn't stop working on his team's cars. Drag racer Don Garlits built his own Swamp Rats.

Many racers enjoy working on the machines almost as much as driving them; anyway, for most beginners, turning their own wrenches is the only way they're going to get to turn a wheel.

Decades ago, driving cross-country to cover some race or other, I made a midnight meal stop in the Midwest. Outside the diner was a Formula Ford on a trailer behind a station wagon, and it wasn't hard to find the racer—he was the only other customer in the place. He told me he was on his way to a race weekend of his own and, yes, he was racing solo. He'd be preparing and servicing his car as well as driving it. And he'd be pounding the Interstate again all Sunday night to make it to work Monday morning.

Even in those days, when a presentable Can-Am team consisted of two mechanics and maybe an engine man, plus a gofer if they were really flush, I marveled at this FF racer's solitary devotion to his sport. But of course he wasn't unusual, not then and I'm sure not now.

Many top mechanics had a dreaming-of-driving phase before hearing their true calling. Chaparral's Franz Weis was one. Another is stock car crew chief Robby Loomis, who recently remarked on TV that he tried the cockpit but decided he showed more promise in the pits. There are lots of former drivers who now crew for their sons or daughters.

Some mechanics have achieved nearly as much renown as their drivers. Alf Francis was a legend behind Stirling Moss. Clint Brawner built the Hawks that Mario Andretti drove to early fame. Ermanno Cuoghi always seemed to be a principle figure in John Wyer's Ford and Porsche teams, and then at Ferrari in the Niki Lauda era. Jo Ramirez held similar positions with Wyer, Gurney, and Tyrrell in my day, and for others long after—he's only just retired. Tyler Alexander

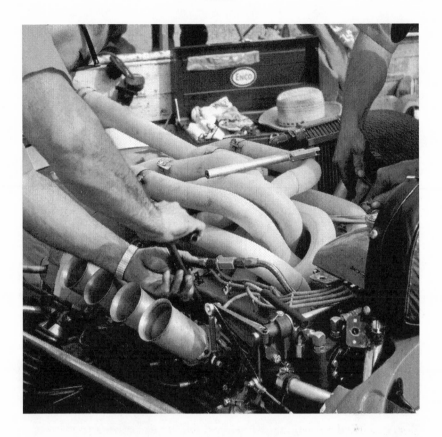

was Bruce McLaren's first mechanic, I believe, and last I heard he's still at McLaren, though at a level way above mechanic.

Often while chatting with these guys, I find remarkable human beings inside the coveralls. Another Chaparral man, Troy Rogers, made Western-themed paintings. McLaren's Alexander is a fine photographer. One day a Lotus F1 crewman told me he wrote poetry. At USAC races, Larry Burton used to awe us all by his ability to work as hard as if he weren't confined to a wheelchair. (Apparently Indy cars weren't enough of a challenge. I last saw him crewing on giant Reno air race warbirds.)

Another thing I notice about mechanics is the great time they're having, even when everything is going badly. They know their work matters, and they take fierce pride in it.

Modestly, I can claim some experience as a race mechanic. Very modestly; I was terrible at it. One time my brother-in-law, Jim McHenry, entered his Datsun 510 in an IMSA support race at Daytona, and I served as his crew so my sister, Claire, could concentrate on timing and lap-charting. My big job was refueling mid-race. I neglected to practice the maneuver, so when I tried to stick the big NASCAR gas churn—say, those suckers are *heavy*—into the rear-mounted filler, I wasn't ready for the little sedan to roll away from me. I felt I was starring in a "Candid Camera" sketch.

I blundered into embarrassment again at Mid-Ohio, where fellow writer Paul Van Valkenburgh was competing in the Trans-Am with a Camaro (which he drove to and from the races, no trailer necessary) and talked me into being his pit crew for the weekend. My inadequacy this time fell in the area of fastidiousness. By pure bad luck we were pitted right next to the Penske team. And it started raining. Filth quickly accumulated on my shapeless T-shirt like grey spray paint, but somehow, uncannily, the Captain's guys' crisp white uniforms remained clean and tidy. I've never felt grubbier in my life.

More happy was a recent experience as the third member of a team competing in a seven-day NASA Track Day with a Subaru WRX. Don Alexander and Rick Herrick were real drivers and also real mechanics, so my sad lack of aptitude in either area did not seriously handicap us. In fact, I discovered a latent knack for cleaning brake dust off wheels. Pretty soon they promoted me to schlepping gas. By week's end I had been dispatched off-site to fetch a vital part, and tasted the thrill of real gofering accomplishment.

Having watched the best at work, I know that mechanicking is far too simple a term for what they do. In times of yore, when even big teams were small, mechanics literally did everything. The real masters could build the car—often to their own design—as well as the engine, tune the whole package like a high-strung piano, and keep the driver's brain on the cam too. That's why Indy cars and others used to have the chief mechanic's name on the cowl right under the driver's. On many cars it probably ought to have been above.

But I once noticed a mechanic, who after all is the one responsible for painting those names, get the last laugh. A car's driver, crew chief and owner were listed in a neat column, driver on top in the time-honored way, but instead of the conventional descriptions the three individuals were identified as "BENDER, MENDER, SPENDER."

Humor blended with truth; to me it said it all about racing mechanics.

19

Jenks and the Mille Miglia

Vintage Racecar, May 2000

HERE'S A SURE BET: a lot of what you know about the Mille Miglia, and most of how you feel about it, came through the writings of a short, towering genius of a journalist named Denis Jenkinson.

Can there be any racing enthusiast who has not thrilled to the epic account "Jenks" penned after riding to victory around a thousand miles of Italian road alongside Stirling Moss?

The race was on May Day, 1955. Jenkinson had been a racer himself—the 1949 world co-champion as a motorcycle sidecar passenger—but had redirected his deep passion for all of motorsport into writing about it. However, it was not for the publicity that Moss asked Jenks along on the Mille Miglia. He simply thought the man's proven nerveless equanimity under stress could help him win.

It was a time in road racing that, today, we must look off-road to see, a Valkyrian time when racing was still done on everyday highways, town to town; when sports racing cars were genuine two-seaters; when the crewmember in the death seat was no mere quavering sack of terror, but an eager participant in the epic contest.

Moss was a young Grand Prix driver for Mercedes-Benz. The factory was also in sports car racing that year, using a variant of its exotic straight-8, fuel-injected, desmodromic-valve Formula 1 machine called the 300 SLR.

Jenks with Brian Redman at Watkins Glen, 1970.

Most of the season's racing was around and around relatively short, closed circuits which could soon be learned. By stark contrast the Mille Miglia, like today's Baja or Dakar desert runs, was a one-lap, presenting the driver a steady stream of all-new problems as fast as the car could go. In the case of the 296-horsepower 300 SLR, that could be better than 170 mph. Moss realized he could use some help.

For weeks ahead of the race the pair pre-ran the course over and over again. Sitting placidly at Moss' side for 10,000 miles of high-speed reconnaissance runs in Mercedes sedans and road-going 300 SL coupes, the journalist painstakingly noted down every significant reference point around the whole course: which way the narrow, two-lane road went after blind corners and hill brows and hump-back bridges, those turns that looked faster than they were, ones that looked slow but weren't. Mindful of the deafening environment of the open race car cockpit, the pair worked out a code of hand signals.

Jenks painstakingly transcribed all this information onto a single 16-foot scroll of paper, and encased it in a custom-made box under a glass window.

On race day the glistening silver Mercedes monster wore a red-painted number 722, for the time of the morning it would charge down the starting ramp at Brescia, heading for Rome. Moss had told Jenkinson that he was going to take the first 200 miles easily, but "he did nothing of the sort," the reporter wrote later. "From the fall of the flag he was driving in a motor race, and he drove to the limit of the conditions at all times. When he was passed briefly by Castellotti he went even faster."

What a ride that was. Flat-out on the long straights beside the Adriatic, Jenkinson watched in awe as the 300 SLR overhauled an aircraft. He held his breath as a sharp rise launched the car airborne too. The noise, the violence, the excitement combined with a bad night cost him his breakfast over the side; afterward he felt better.

He made one mistake: distracted by fuel sloshing onto his neck right after a stop, he neglected to signal a nasty turn. They just scraped through.

Moss also erred, three times crinkling the aluminum nose on hay bales, once narrowly missing a house. At another point a grabbing drum brake spun the Mercedes into a ditch. But when they arrived at Rome, they were leading the race. As they accelerated away northbound, Jenks later wrote, Moss "metaphorically spat on his hands and 'tigered' for the next 450 miles all the way back to Brescia determined, having got the lead, to hold on to it—Fangio, Taruffi, Kling, Maglioli, come who may."

Powering through throngs of suicidally excited villagers, throwing the big car over tortuous mountain passes and across bucolic river valleys, streaking at up to 175 mph past stone walls and power poles, olive groves and vineyards, farms and factories, Moss and Jenkinson shot under the finish flag after 10 hours and seven minutes of open-bore, open-road racing. They had set segment records all the way along, and only just missed averaging 100 mph for the whole distance.

Does such a tale get your blood up? It does mine. I was raised on Denis Jenkinson. As a speed-mad teen I tried to find everything he ever wrote, and read it again and again. I poured over his classic 1958 book, *The Racing Driver*, until I could quote it (though I did carefully take the quotes above from the original). It wasn't just stories, it was science. Knowledge. Understanding. Truth.

This Jenkinson guy was doing what I wanted to do. So I did. One grand day I found myself prowling the same pit lanes. Jenks turned out to be as engaging in person as in print. The first time we spoke was at Spa during the 1000K in 1972. I was astride a Honda 750, and this lifelong British Bikie came over, fascinated by the big Japanese Four.

Fascinated, and a little bemused; he found a way to poke fun at its complexity. Pointing to the row of indicator lights on the dash, he asked in his deep, deep voice, "What about all these, then?" I demonstrated each one's function. "Ooooh," he said, his eyes twinkling merrily. "Can you get 'em all goin' at once?"

Jenks was a short person, but you never saw him low. One year at the Monaco GP a crowd of press persons upset about something or other was having a crowded, noisy meeting, and Denis put in a point. "Speak up, speak up!" came a cry from the back of the throng. Without an instant's hesitation, the gnome-like figure popped up onto a chair. Everyone cheered.

Gnomes, you'll remember from your Tolkien, are tough. I recall a pit lane tut-tut over the latest scandal about Lotus' Colin Chapman. Jenks inhaled sharply, drew himself up, and roared fiercely, "If you say a word against him, I shall knock you down!"

Stories of Jenkinsonian eccentricities are legion. They say he lived alone in a small country cottage, where he ran the lights off a wheezy generator with barely enough power to illuminate one bulb at a time. A dinner guest tells of sitting at the kitchen table, but being taken aback when his host remained standing at the stove, eating from the pan. "Why don't you sit down, Denis?" the guest ventured. "You've got the plate," was the matter-of-fact reply.

But the man wrote magic. He left us enriched. I never got to the Mille Miglia, but he took me there. It's a sure thing that, if I ever had a guru in this business, Jenks was it.

Alfred Momo, Cunningham chief mechanic, takes a Maserati to the start at Sebring, 1955.

Section 2

Cars

20

Aston Imprints

Vintage Racecar, June 2009

Le Mans champion Roy Salvadori once wrote in a UK magazine, decades ago, about driving his winning Aston Martin DBR1 on the open English road. One could take such liberties there in those green and pleasant days of yore.

"This is a car you'd better have pointed in the right direction when you pull the trigger," is my recollection of what he said.

Good old Salvo's indelible words about that marvelously potent and regally beautiful sports racer would have forever stamped the Aston Martin marque on my soul, but in fact it had already happened. I believe a DB3 coupe first imprinted itself on me half a dozen years earlier.

I'm a sucker for a pretty body, anybody's, but that British lady's face also sparkled with intelligence and character, and she smoldered with internal fire, hidden below a cool grace that struck me dumb. I probably felt like bowing. I know I longed to hold her hand.

Astons have been doing that to me ever since. The striking coupe gave birth to an even more stunning racing roadster, the DB3S. She first caught my eye on magazine covers, then as she sped by on the track or rested, demurely, in paddocks I stalked.

But it was another published story that really set my senses seething. *Autosport's* John Bolster road tested a racing DB3S out on

Aston Martin DB9R at Sebring, 2005.

the public highway, and came back raving about its balance, obedience, and eager speed.

"I can imagine nothing more delectable," I remember him musing, "than a DB3S fitted with a snug little hood against the icy blast and the roads of the Continent before me." (A "hood" is a top, to us non-Brits.)

Years later I finally lived that dream for myself, if not with an Aston. I bought a new Stingray Corvette and took it to Europe for endless summers of Grand Prix racing. A crazy stunt, but John Bolster made me do it.

Even more gorgeous than the DB3S were Aston Martin's sports racers of the late 1950s, the DBR2s we saw in the States and the DBR1 that Salvadori drove with Carroll Shelby to win Le Mans in 1959. To my eye, these cars rate among the most achingly appealing of all time.

I wasn't at Le Mans for the great Aston victory, but it was at Le Mans that I had my defining DBR1 moment. To enliven the modern Audi race the clever French also put on a vintage event, and the 1959 winner was there. But it was away from the track, in heavy city traffic, that my rapture hit me.

There I was, inching along in my loaner Fiat, bored and broiling in the afternoon heat, when I heard a heavy rasp and saw a flash of pale green in the side mirror. Under my elbow shot that iconic shape, heading boldly up the oncoming lane like a shark hunting herring.

No, I have no idea why an open-pipe racing car was carving up a French city. It's enough that I can still hear the glorious baritone of the straight-six echoing off the ornate building facades even after the ageless warrior was long gone from sight.

The special thing for me about Aston Martin is that, somehow, through changes of ownership and personnel and economic fortune, they've been making their new cars as alluring as my old heartthrobs. Their street cars still turn my head, every time, and during ALMS races a few seasons back, I would stand transfixed by the sleek DBR9 coupes, impatient on every lap for them to spear into sight again. My lens loved their lines. My ears loved the sweet trumpet's blare from their V-12s. They even gushed fire from their sidepipes. Oh, yes, they won races, too!

Beauty, brains, and sleek athletic prowess. Passion breathing softly into my ear in a cultivated English accent. Pardon me, I must go sit, my knees are weak.

This was written for a Vintage Racecar *special issue honoring Aston Martin.*

21

See the Chaparrals!

Vintage Racecar, July 2004

SPEAKING IN A ROOM packed with eager ears, Vic Elford was well launched into a detailed description of how he used to drive the Chaparral 2J's "automatic" transmission way back in 1970, when he abruptly paused.

Poker-faced, he turned to the long-secretive creator of the fabulous Road Runners, who was standing nearby, hearing everything.

"Uhm . . . Jim," said Vic. "Is it all right, now, to . . ."

Tall Jim Hall tried to hold back a smile. "Well, you're already halfway through tellin' it anyway!" Their audience roared.

This had been a long time coming—more than 40 years. In the old days, Chaparral mechanics would work under tarps to hide their torque-converter gearboxes from prying eyes. But at last the secrets are out. Not only out, but on open display and even freely explained.

Trick transmissions, flipper-wings, ground-effect aerodynamics, and composite chassis construction; it's all laid bare in a beautiful, spacious hall of memories called the Chaparral Gallery in Midland, Texas. The world's most innovative series of sports-racing cars is now permanently safeguarded and showcased here, just five miles up the road from the famous Rattlesnake Raceway, where they were born.

Lorna and I were at the grand opening, where the above exchange took place during a forum before 200 fans. Though I had the honor of

Chaparral 2E debuts The Wing at Bridgehampton, 1966.

moderating the forum, which I suppose casts my objectivity in doubt, I sincerely recommend the long trip to see the Gallery. In fact, I predict this new, $7.6-million addition to Midland's Petroleum Museum is going to become a point of pilgrimage for racing enthusiasts and automotive engineering students from around the globe. (Info at www. petroleummuseum.org or call 432-683-4403.)

Every surviving Chaparral 2 sports-racer is here. There's one of the trio of original mid-engined roadsters with glass-fiber monocoques, which Jim Hall drove to the United States Road Racing Championship in 1964, and with which he and partner Hap Sharp won the Sebring 12 Hour in 1965.

Standing by also are the chassis of the other two roadsters, which were later rebodied as coupes; one's a 2D and the other a 2F, winners of international enduros in 1966 and 1967, respectively.

Then there's a 2E Can-Am car, which introduced the high, suspension-mounted wing in 1966; the lone 2H "quasi-coupe," 1969's unloved experiment in ultra-low drag; and Elford's 2J, the following year's Ground Effects Vehicle, or "Fan Car," which was promptly banned.

Even an example of the 1980 Indy-winning Chaparral 2K is on display, hung high so you can study its underbody tunnels.

Only two type-2 models are missing, and only because they no longer exist. The 2C of 1965, the first car with driver-variable downforce, was turned into the first 2E. The 2G, built from the second E, was destroyed in Hall's career-ending crash at Las Vegas in 1968.

Nor are any of the front-engined type 1s included. Jim long ago sold his pair, and doesn't feel those Troutman & Barnes-built California specials were really his cars anyway.

Besides the cars, the professionally designed museum displays include well-written descriptive panels, evocative period photos and, my special favorites, action models to demonstrate how Chaparral wings and fans generated downforce.

A full-size mockup of a 2E invites visitors to step aboard and use their left feet to operate the wing's flipper-pedal. There's also a movie alcove showing Chaparrals in action, an automotive fine arts gallery, and of course a gift shop offering Chaparral-themed apparel, books and models.

If you can tear yourself away from all that, the other part of the Petroleum Museum tells the rich story of the industry in which Jim Hall and Hap Sharp made their wealth, hence making the Chaparrals possible.

Pete shows Lorna how The Wing works at Midland, 2004.

But I was fixated on the cars. So few of them! As often before, I was struck by how much history was made with so little equipment. When they were racing, there seemed to be multitudes of these exotic, mysterious machines from faraway West Texas, something new every race. But in reality Chaparral was a small and frugal team, continually altering one car to make a new model.

Another renewed revelation came during a side trip to Rattlesnake Raceway. All those incredible cars came out of an astonishingly modest compound of small steel buildings, little more than sheds. The adjoining private test track—Chaparral's secret weapon of the 1960s—is a two-mile loop of asphalt (now seriously degrading) that looks narrow, bumpy, and scarily primitive to modernized eyes.

And the staff? Asked about the highest number of people who ever worked here, Chaparral's master fabricator Troy Rogers thought back a moment and said, "Counting Jim and [his wife] Sandy, thirteen."

Of course, added to that would be a visiting population of Chaparral's special friends, the engineers at Chevrolet who supplied truckloads of experimental hardware and man-years of priceless expertise. Jim Hall addressed that clandestine connection with GM during the forum. He pointed out that, while the automaker had a no-racing policy at the time, the engineers weren't really racing. They were simply watching as Chaparral raced, putting Chevy's ideas to the ultimate performance test.

That forum itself was something special. On what other occasion would you see gathered at one table the likes of Jim Hall, Chaparral crew chief Franz Weis, their drivers Gil de Ferran, Bob Donner, Vic Elford, Phil Hill, Ronnie Hissom, and Brian Redman, *plus* rival driver/constructor Dan Gurney? It was a magic couple of hours, over far too soon.

But the cars remain, and they'll be there forever, mythic machines long hidden, now bathed in spotlights. Yes, Midland in West Texas is a long way from just about anywhere, but remember, remoteness is part of the Chaparral story. Really, the Chaparral Gallery is a must-see.

22

The Immortal Cobra

Vintage Racecar, June 2010

THERE WAS A SUMMER of my life when I often walked back home from an evening ramble in a European city to the outlying village where I had a job in a sawmill. A lengthy stretch of the way was dead straight and lit in the eerie orange of sodium vapor lamps. This road was almost always deserted that late at night, and frequently the air was misty, so the long line of lights faded away into nothingness both before me and behind. It was like floating in a void, removed from reality.

Naturally, my mind kept dwelling on Cobras.

Carroll Shelby's masterpiece was just out that summer, and though I hadn't seen one yet, I'd been devouring every word and picture I could find. I was sure I knew all about this thrilling new sports car that was tearing up race tracks everywhere. A least I knew enough to know it was the sports car I really, truly wanted.

As I strode along under those endless street lamps, I kept visualizing me driving a Cobra instead, booting it flat-out on that empty straightaway, roaring through the pools of orange illumination so fast they would blend into a staccato flickering.

One never wants to lose a fantasy like that, and to this day a fevered corner of my brain still holds an image of a 289 Cobra as the perfectly proportioned sports roadster. Specifically, the FIA racing model. I happened to gaze upon one of these again recently, and yup. Perfect.

But I don't want a real one. Too pricey, but also too priceless. I'd rather have a version built from a kit, so I could personalize it as I pleased (seating, instrument layout, maybe a sleeker windscreen) without having to worry about the authenticity police.

Of all the nutty urges I get, building my own kit car is one of the zaniest. Yet, while most of my romantic notions fall away with time (no longer do I seriously wish to bicycle around the world, for example), I've never shaken this thing about the Cobra.

Nor have innumerable others, to judge from the incredible number of replicas and quasi-replicas we still see on the market and

Sebring, 1964.

on car show fields. Backgrounding this phenomenon is that Shelby made only about a thousand real ones, and they trade for hundreds of thousands of dollars.

Yet limited production has not been enough to bestow immortality on any number of other automobiles. I wonder why this one little roadster, quirky, cramped, cranky in many ways, has such sticking power in our hearts.

Certainly it's not a sophisticated driving machine like, say, a Porsche or a Lotus of its time. Look at the Cobra and those scattered gauges. Upright seats. Offset footwell. Soft aluminum body with jokes for bumpers. That archaic leaf-spring suspension!

Really, the 289 is a Yankee hot-rod, a forced transatlantic marriage of an AC Ace—a car I admired in its Bristol-engined form—with a massive iron Ford V-8. How could *that* work?

Well, of course it worked beautifully, thanks to Shelby's vision and determination and the expert development work carried out by masters such as Ken Miles (something of an Anglo-American hybrid himself). When I finally made my way to places Cobras were racing—Bridgehampton, Sebring, and Watkins Glen—they were doing nothing but winning.

See what racing heritage will do for a car? Suppose Ol' Shel had never thought of sending his lil' Cobra into open combat against 'Vettes and GTOs and the like. Had his ambition stretched only to a stylish street cruiser, no matter how good the end product, do you believe you'd know its name today?

But by racing his Cobra, Shelby built a brand that will live on long after any of us.

As confessed above, I was already a Cobra a fan when at last I got my hands on one. Real life experience carries the danger that it can destroy a dream, but this was one time it didn't. The car I drove was a new 289 street model that a friend named Kenny Krieger brought to my parents' Pennsylvania home one night.

It had been raining, and the loop of roads around the neighborhood was still wet. Perfect conditions for trying out a powerful two-seater.

I must have settled in and felt at home immediately, for I remember booting the tail out as early as the second corner. On and on I went, powerslide after powerslide, small-block Ford bellowing madly, turning lap after lusty lap of mom and dad's otherwise quiet little housing tract, Kenny sitting comfortably and pridefully alongside, until halfway around lap four our headlights picked out a waving yellow. A rain slicker in the clenched fists of a very irate neighbor. So I didn't do a lap five.

Nor has an opportunity come along to drive another Cobra. But I still know I want one. Why?

Size is a major element of it. This is a pure sports car no bulkier than it needs to be. No fat on the muscle. Like a race car.

Simplicity is another part of the appeal. A person really can build one at home. Cobras know nothing of complex subsystems or accessories. They're just eight cylinders, four tires, two seats and a gearstick. Worried about temperature control or baggage capacity or your hairstyle? Take the minivan.

And speed, of course. Nowadays, all these years later, there are many faster vehicles to buy, but I really don't know how much speed you need. Seems to me, if you can lift the nose and slide the tail and get the neighbors riled up, you're riding enough horse.

So that's why, if you look over my shoulder, you may catch me surfing Cobra kit Web sites. My bucket list says I still have some street lamps to blur.

The village was Zaandam, near Amsterdam. I'd arrived there on a bicycle and stopped to make more money for the next leg of a projected ride around the world. Which I never completed. It dawned on me that when you were in the Netherlands, everywhere else was uphill.

23

Ferrari in the Grass

Vintage Racecar, April 1999

JUST AS THE SUN was setting at Daytona I went out hunting, and the very first trophy I bagged was a Ferrari Corsa. It was at rest but alert in yellowed grass, long red body poised on springy wire wheels. It seemed to be suspiciously sniffing the other vintage cars clustered with it in this fenced compound like diverse animals at a waterhole. They all seemed to be listening nervously to the raging sounds of modern wildlife racing around the Speedway close outside.

Slowly, I drew my pen. I hadn't known quite what I was after, but I knew this was more than I'd hoped for.

What an extraordinary time we enthusiasts live in. Our technology has reached the point that it can be used against itself, to relieve the emotional dislocation it has caused us. The very science that has been whiplashing us numb by its ever-accelerating pace, now is capable of restoring and even recreating cherished icons of our past, to give us back some of our stability.

We aren't built for rapid change, we upright anthropoids. We cope with it, perhaps even enjoy the thrill, but too much progress too fast pulls our roots out. I don't know how your ride through life is going, but for me lately, it's been like the throttle's jammed open and the rev limiter's broke.

One important thing vintage racing gives me is a sense of speed control. That's what I saw in that lovely, lovingly renewed, 50-year-old

Ferrari. Almost as old as I, it linked me directly to myself at the age when I began to see meaning in cars and racing.

Here, unedited, is what I scribbled in my little notebook that balmy January evening, as I took a break from the cloying Media Center and ventured out to find something real to write about:

"At dusk I tire of trying to fill in data blanks, and take a walk to soak up atmosphere in soft evening light and air. In HSR area of infield I see several cars on display atop scanty Florida shortgrass, just like old Sebring, and there is Corsa Ferrari. I have a memory moment: rich guys of my childhood—1940s-50s—hunched over these open air steering wheels, thrashing around makeshift courses. The technology has changed, but not the soul.

"I make right wander, and am there when Corsa owner fires it up and drives away—click-tickticktick, whirrr-blattblattblatt—crisp."

My juices up, I wandered on and came across other, more pertinent things to put in my story about the 24-hour race. But I can't get that old Ferrari out of my mind, nor do I want to.

An awkward young colt of a car, a simple cigar slung between cycle fenders, it was old-fashioned the day it rasped to life in Ferrari's factory courtyard. Maranello soon birthed more sophisticated models. The Corsa was edged into retirement.

But not into oblivion. I believe vintage racing saved it.

No, not right away. In those days, a race car's life span was determined by its competitiveness. When something like this Ferrari dropped back from the front lines, usually it was sent elsewhere to race, changing hands and venues and sometimes engines again and again, until finally it was obsolete everywhere.

Then, if it wasn't left to corrode away behind some shed, it might be granted mummification in a museum. If really lucky, it found respectful hands to restore it to original condition, even to running condition.

Devotion to historic machinery is nothing new. When I was a kid, my dad took me to numerous classic car "meets" for vehicles that to me, then, looked as ancient as sailing ships. Like surviving tall ships,

The Corsa with other Ferraris (and a Jag) at Bridgehampton, 1952.

they were capable of careful exercise. Once, indeed, famous motoring writer Ken Purdy gave me a ride atop his equally famous old Mercer Raceabout. A pretty brisk ride, in fact. I remember being startled by cold air blowing up my pants legs.

Who knows, maybe clambering aboard Mr. Purdy's yellow speedster was my first step to wandering the Daytona infield these four decades later.

What's different about the old car world now? It's no longer a quiet, cautious backwater. Enthusiasm for vintage racing has been explosive, and one consequence has been to make old cars new.

Literally, in some cases. Audi's construction of a new Auto Union chassis simply stunned me when I saw it run at Goodwood last summer, and that was before the driver burned donuts with it. No fear, now Audi's even making a brand new V-16 motor. We'll hear it at Monterey. Here is an example of the highest automotive technology of one of the great Golden Ages, an achievement that had required big government backing of a major automaker. Yet today, a private workshop can build the same machine.

Do you suppose one day any high school science class will be able to turn out Saturn V moon rockets?

Anyway, custodians of precious old cars no longer need to fear firing them up because something irreplaceable might break. First of all, thanks to the vintage racing community's dedication, skill, and ever-growing knowledge, breakage is more likely to be avoided. And if not, the piece probably can be duplicated. In the same way that historic images originally made on fragile film are now being safely preserved through computer technology, great race cars that used to sit mute can freely roar again.

Vintage events aren't like musty trophy rooms anymore. We get the whole living, Jurassic Park experience.

I feel my white knuckles relaxing.

24

Ginther's Honda

Vintage Racecar, April 2011

THE SOUND STOPPED ME in my shoes. A wild shriek spearing out of the new Japanese F1 sliced like a samurai sword through the dronings and raspings of the commonplace European engines. "Beware!" that unearthly cry proclaimed, "We are coming."

It was at Watkins Glen in 1964, the next to last year of the 1.5-liter formula. Honda, an established force in motorcycles, was new to cars. But hubris said, why not jump in at the top?

Inspired, led, and sometimes brusquely goaded by Soichiro Honda himself, young engineers and technicians drew up and constructed their own F1 engine, an astonishingly ambitious V-12. That came to 125cc per jewel-like cylinder. Like the latest Euro-engines, it packed four valves into each combustion chamber. Unlike them, it sat crosswise in the chassis, motorcycle-fashion.

Also setting this newcomer apart was its horsepower. Already it made 210 or so at 11,800 rpm, thought to be among the highest in F1, but Mr. Honda demanded more. Back in 1962 he himself had set the original project designation: RA270. The numbers were said to be his ultimate horsepower target. Hubris, and a constant spur to his sleep-deprived staff.

A racer in his youth, the company founder even ceremoniously drove the first car on its first lap at his factory's research center. Can you imagine a parallel in today's F1?

Jack Brabham also tested that car, and would go on to win many F2 races with smaller Honda engines, but if he had any idea of building an F1 program around the V-12, he chose against it. (His Oldsmobile-based Repco V-8s would do the job well enough.)

That first car was an early 1963 test bed built along the lines of a space-frame Cooper that Honda had acquired. Meanwhile, a deal with Lotus was supposed to bring a modern monocoque chassis, but when that fell through Mr. Honda directed his youngsters to fold-up their own aluminum tub. This new car's designation was RA271. That much more pressure on the dyno guys.

Another Honda departure from F1 norms was its choice of driver. Instead of hiring an experienced European veteran, they surprised both the world and an American club racer named Ronnie Bucknum. A winner in MGB production cars, he had never driven an open-wheeler.

His first ever Grand Prix was on the Nürburgring—all 14.2 miles and 174 turns of it. Mechanical trouble forced a start from the back, but he was up to 11th when he spun and crashed.

Ginther touch-tests exhaust temps at Watkins Glen, 1965.

At Monza Bucknum qualified 10th, out of 20 on the grid, and got to 7th before retiring with brake trouble.

Soichiro Honda came to Watkins Glen. I met him there, sort of. My sister, Claire, was the family star that evening in the garage. She already owned one of his motorcycles (preceding me by six years), so our dad, Ozzie, boldly propelled her toward the exotic Asian visitor and blurted out, "Mr. Honda, this is my daughter, she rides Honda."

The manufacturer smiled warmly at her, bowed deeply and said, "Tenk you ver' much!"

Ronnie Bucknum qualified 14th at the Glen and went out once more, this time with engine trouble. Three races and three retirements that first year, but the Honda team was learning a lot. For 1965 they further tweaked the screaming V-12, paring weight and boosting power to 230 at 13,000. They also built a stiffer, more refined monocoque. This was the RA272.

Another change in 1965: Honda hired a second driver, one with F1 experience at both Ferrari and BRM. Richie Ginther, Bucknum's fellow Californian, was a former mechanic who was known as a strong development driver. One day at Ferrari, testing a new sports prototype that was persistently unstable, he thought back to his time as a military airframe mechanic and riveted on what he called a trim tab. Presto, Richie Ginther invented the tail spoiler.

Many years later, at his beachside home in Baja, Richie told me of joining Honda. His ginger temperament clashed with both Enzo Ferrari and the management of BRM, and he'd stalked out of those teams. As he put it to me, "If someone didn't have an open mind, I was of no value to them."

But he found the perfect environment at Honda, a manufacturer that understood and valued him, and that had both the open-mindedness and the resources to act on his advice.

"The Honda was damned good for a first effort, but it was kind of sorrowful to see some of the things that could be done for it.

"It turned out to be rather difficult for Ronnie. But he had gone from MGBs straight into F1. He had the Honda F1 car handling like a production car. It was too soft in roll, so you had to wait to get it into a turn."

Ginther persuaded the techs to stiffen the suspension, and soon was rewarding them with much faster times around Suzuka. "By the end of the test two or three days later, the difference was something ridiculous, into the teens of seconds. They were getting drunk on 'what-ifs.' Everybody was happy except Ronnie. He was taking it personally, but it really wasn't his fault, dammit."

In their turn, the Honda guys showed Ginther what they were made of at the Belgian GP, the first of the '65 season. During practice the crankshafts broke in both cars. "It was a design fault," Richie explained. "Those suckers designed and sent three new cranks over as excess passenger baggage!

"Oh, those Honda people. Japanese people are the smartest people I've ever worked with. One time they asked me to draw the engine power curve I wanted on a greenboard. I said, 'Take 10 off the top, but give me 20 mid-range.' They gave me the 20, but without losing any at the top. They were very pleased with that.

"I felt incompetent as far as engines were concerned when I was around those people. It was a delight."

In the Belgian race Ginther went on to give Honda its first world championship point, scoring a sixth in his debut for the team. On through the rest of the season the little V-12 often showed winning speed, particularly at the starts of races. But it seldom ran well to the end, as temperature buildup robbed power.

Until the last GP of the year—and of the 1500 formula—at the high altitude of Mexico City.

"They had changed something in the fuel injection, what I'm not certain. It was their own system. We'd been there a week ahead of time, which really helped a lot. We got the mixture and the chassis right." He qualified on the second row.

"I got off with the other cars, but started to fade as I didn't get quite enough wheelspin to get the engine up on step. I dipped the clutch, got wheelspin, and I shot ahead between Dan Gurney and Jimmy Clark so fast I sat up from my reclining position and looked over at Dan with a big grin on my face. He was surprised. I looked over at Jimmy, too, but he was looking straight ahead. I came off the line like a dragster. Out of the third turn I looked in my mirrors and I thought, 'There's been an accident.'"

There wasn't, of course. Ginther's Honda was simply that much faster.

"The chassis and engine worked superbly. One change I had been asking for, we now had at Mexico, a fuel mixture control. After a few laps a pit signal says, 'Put it rich.' It cost about 300 rpm on the straight, but I'm still out front and holding my own.

"I came up to lap Brabham on the straight behind the pits. He was going slowly, the SOB, waiting for me. They don't call him Black Jack for nothing. He moved over right, then left. I had to brake and change down a couple of gears. I stood on it, he did too, it was a drag race. I didn't put my brake on until I was past him, and took the high line into the banked turn before the pits where Ricardo [Rodriguez] was killed, a no-no. I went around driving with one hand and giving him the bird. There's a bad bump off the banking and I just brushed the wall at the exit with the rear wheel.

"But it was the day for that car."

For both RA272s. Teammate Bucknum screamed home fifth. And Honda, into F1 history.

25

In the Beginning, There Was the C-type

Vintage Racecar, September 2010

THE STEERING FEEL; that's what I remember best. The pinion perfectly meshing with its rack was a tactile delight in my fingers, giving a sense of well-bedded and properly oiled Olde English machinery cheery in its work.

Second impression: the way that long, lazy-seeming six awakened at 3000 rpm and eagerly rushed toward 5500, expressing its joy-of-life with a raucous rasp exploding from the over-under exhaust barrels just over the side of the open cockpit.

I was nicely nested in stout steel tubing, my eyes feasting on sweet aluminum body curves, my scalp delighting in the airblast over the low windscreen. All right, the seating space was short, forcing my spine more upright than I like and buckling my knees a little.

But I was in a forgiving mood. As a youth I'd watched C-types racing and longed one day to drive one. Thanks to Steve Earle, longtime owner of chassis number 50 (of 54 total), I finally had the opportunity. It was worth the wait.

The C-type was Jaguar's first racing car, and a sensational one. Built for Le Mans in 1951, it won there in its racing debut. Two years later it triumphed again, this time introducing disc brakes.

Moving rapidly, Jaguar then launched the D-type, a much more sophisticated design with greater speed that would win the French classic a further three times and leave the poor old C-type looking old- fashioned.

But that's not a fair way to remember any pioneer. In its time, the C was the finest competition instrument Jaguar engineers could produce, and it beat the world's best. Twice. Its success blazed the trail that other Jaguars would follow. They may have been better, but only because they came along later. Without the C, they might not have come at all.

But the Jaguar C-type deserves our appreciation not only because it was first, but because it was unique. In 1951 Englishmen were still

"C-Jag" at the Giants Despair hill climb, 1955.

cleaning up war rubble and denying themselves luxuries, and their auto industry was working hard merely to get production going again, let alone develop new models.

It that circumstance, it's astonishing that company founder William Lyons and his merry men launched, not just a new line of Jaguar cars, but one so technically advanced. Their 3.4-liter twin-cam XK engine—designed for sedans but introduced in 1948's XK120 sports car—was a wonder of the day.

Surely it would have been enough to take the sports car to Le Mans in essentially standard form, just to prove the product, and that's just what Jaguar did in 1950. But something went wrong: The team's trio of XK120s showed more speed than expected. By noon on Sunday one car was running in second place—and lapping faster than the eventual winner, a 4.5-liter, Grand Prix-based Talbot.

Clutch failure ended that thrill, but the other two Jaguars finished the 24 hours, placing 12th and 15th. The normally cautious, conservative William Lyons found himself love-struck by Le Mans. He authorized his team to come back the following year with purpose-built racing cars. He meant to win the bally race.

Again, Jaguar might have done the bare minimum, and indeed Lyons had his boys start work on a trio of modified XK120s with lightened chassis frames and magnesium bodywork. But these LT models were only for backup, and in the end weren't needed because the pure racers turned out so well.

Though its official designation, XK120C, implied a "competition" version of the standard sports car, the C-type was as far removed from the production line as any Le Mans Ferrari of the period. In fact, Jaguar's chassis design was more advanced than a contemporary Ferrari's, more of a true space-frame with tubing ranging between one and two inches in diameter. Steel firewall and rear bulkhead panels welded into place stiffened the structure, foreshadowing the D-type's full monocoque design.

That bulkhead behind the cockpit was basically the back end of the chassis, with the rear suspension links cantilevered rearward from it. Rather than hang the rear axle on leaf springs, as on the road model, the C-type used a transverse torsion bar.

Since the axle didn't have a limited-slip differential, the suspension geometry included an interesting angled arm running back to the upper right side of the axle. In a typical live axle, engine torque makes the pinion "climb" the ring gear, thus lifting the right rear wheel and making it more prone to spin. The C-type's link resisted this lifting force, keeping the tire pressed to the road during acceleration.

At the front, independent suspension on longitudinal torsion bars was similar to the XK120's, but the steering was by rack and pinion, not recirculating ball. At 96 inches the race car's wheelbase was six shorter.

Another departure from the Jaguar norm was that the C's handmade aluminum bodywork wasn't styled by William Lyons, but shaped by aerodynamicist Malcolm Sayer. The reason, as chief engineer Bill Heynes joked (?), was that the boss had gone off to America on a sales trip, which had the added benefit of letting the job be completed in record time!

Only one door was let into the body, just a sketchy thing for the right-side driver. Like the D-type (and E-type) to come, the C-type's nosepiece hinged up for good access. Under it stood the magnificent XK engine, its polished aluminum cam covers gleaming proudly. Mildly hopped up, it put out a trifle over 200 horsepower at 5500 rpm. The weight it had to pull was about 2100 pounds, some 30 percent less than the standard XK120. Top speed was more than 140 mph.

Are you unimpressed by these numbers? To the motor racing world of 1951 they were phenomenal. And so was the Jaguar's performance at Le Mans, the most important race on the globe, where the sleek newcomer beat Allards, Aston Martins, Cunninghams, Ferraris, Nash-Healeys, and Talbots to win by 67 miles.

Sure, power, technologies and velocities would rise rapidly through the years to come, led for much of the way by the Cats from Coventry, eventual winners of seven Le Mans enduros in all. But none of those future advances diminish the achievements represented by the seminal C-type.

An early chapter in Jaguar's book of great deeds it may be, but a joy to "read" it is still.

Originally prepared for Vintage Racecar's *special issue marking Jaguar's 75th anniversary, with some information drawn from the author's 1991 marque history,* Jaguar, Performance and Pride, *Publications International.*

26

My Favorite Lotus

Vintage Racecar, October 2002

AMONG THE ARRAY of anniversaries we've been celebrating recently, one is a particular standout for me. It's now 50 years since Colin Chapman founded Lotus Engineering.

What exciting cars that man made!

If you weren't around to experience it, try to imagine the sense of revelation that swept the enthusiast community each time a new Lotus came out. It was like turning a page and discovering The Answer. "Oh! So *that's* how to do it!"

I'll never forget the electric thrill I felt upon my first close look at a Lotus Mark 18, the chunky little open-wheeler that marked Chapman's move to mid-engines. A small-bore version had just been delivered to a Pennsylvania sports car shop I habitually haunted on my way home from work.

This would have been sometime during the winter of 1960-'61, when my enthusiasm was still so fresh I often hobby-designed space frames and suspension layouts (on paper), just to learn how it all worked. I knew the new Lotus was advanced, but seeing it in the metal was exhilarating.

One elegant detail I recall in the front suspension: Where other cars used additional bolts and brackets to mount the anti-roll bar, this one saved weight by conjoining two pivots on one bolt. So simple, so elegant, so right! It so charged me up that I raced on home to drag my dad back to see it that very night.

At that stage, Colin Chapman had been building cars for over 12 years, but was only on the brink of earning his real fame. He'd begun in 1948, while still in engineering school, by hot-rodding an Austin sedan into a trials special, aka "mud plugger." His second model, capable of race track use as well, came in 1950. That's the year he formally started his company in response to customer demand, but it wasn't until 1955 that Chapman felt enough confidence in Lotus' future to give up his day job.

A talented driver himself, Chapman brought to his design work the racer's craving to push every limit. His ideas were always novel and often daring, while his structures were amazingly light—some would say dangerously so. Indeed, Lotus history has more than its share of tragic crashes due to component failure. The cars made many champions (Jim Clark, Graham Hill, Emerson Fittipaldi, Mario Andretti), but in one case honor was posthumous (Jochen Rindt, 1970).

Interested more in innovation than in production, Chapman tended to lose focus on a given project once it was far enough along that he could see the next Big Step. That meant a lot of underdeveloped cars, and not every Lotus was a success. In fact, a few were frankly bad cars.

But so many were immortally great. In Formula 1 trim, that 18 that so excited me quickly became Stirling Moss's weapon of choice, driven to such victories as the 1960 USGP at Riverside (which I had the fortune to witness) and his epic underdog-beats-Ferrari performance at Monaco in 1961, among others.

"Lotuses were never the easiest to drive, [but] they were the best," Moss once explained to me. "[They] were delicate, they were a precision job, and if you had the precision and were very skillful you certainly could do better in them than in any other car."

After Moss retired, the next king of F1 was Jimmy Clark. His brilliant hands got the best out of another breakthrough Chapman car, the Lotus 25 of 1962, which featured F1's first monocoque chassis. In

Emmo in the 72 at Watkins Glen, 1970.

it Clark took the 1963 World Championship, and repeated the feat two years later in a developed version of the same design called the Mk. 33. Also in 1965, Clark won the Indy 500 in a Lotus 38.

I thought those and several other early Lotuses were magnificent designs, but all were knocked aside in my mind by 1967's model 49. Perfection! Ford Cosworth's brand new, ultra-compact DFV was an integral, stress-bearing part of the latest graceful Lotus monocoque. It was a marriage of ideals with a soul-satisfying storybook result: the 49 won its first-ever race. It went on to make Graham Hill champion in 1968, and remained competitive in F1 into 1970, when Rindt won Monaco in the 49's fourth season. Granted, he won because Jack Brabham made a mistake on the last corner of the race, but still, not many Grand Prix cars last as long as the 49.

Busy Lotus was all the way up to Mark number 72 when time finally came for a new F1 model, and what a dramatic new device that 1970 car was.

Too dramatic, for once, for me; I can remember not liking the 72 at first. It looked alien to eyes that loved shapes as smooth as the 49. Chapman and his staff of designers gave their 72 the "door stop" or "racer's wedge" profile of the 1968 Indianapolis Lotus Turbine (Mk. 56), keeping the front-end airflow clean by installing a pair of radiators amidships. That chisel nose made so much downforce that at first the car needed a bulky, three-element "Venetian blind" rear wing, another strange apparition in 1970. Additional features borrowed from the four-wheel-drive Indy car were front driveshafts, in this case hooked only to inboard brakes.

A weird contraption, but effective, though not immediately. Unlike the 49, the 72 didn't win first time out. But Rindt did drive it to victory in the model's third GP, starting from pole, and followed up with three more wins in a row. That made the sensational Austrian the championship points leader going into the Italian GP. There he was killed in practice when one of those front brake shafts snapped and the car veered into a guardrail.

Four weeks afterward Emerson Fittipaldi put the team back on its feet at Watkins Glen, scoring yet another Lotus 72 victory in only his own fourth GP. The result ensured Rindt would be named that year's World Champion. Two years later Emmo achieved his own first F1 title, still driving a 72 for Lotus.

By this time my tastes had caught up to Chapman's imagination, and now I reckoned the Lotus 72 was one of the greatest cars ever, a scientifically beautiful machine that made everything else look archaic. It especially looked that way with Ronnie Petersen hurling it through turns on opposite lock, blue smoke pouring off the rear tires!

It was a dark day for me when tire "improvements" stopped him driving that way.

But "Super Swede" was still winning races in the 72 during 1974, the car's fifth season, and that fact has stayed with me. I fully respect Chapman's next leap forward, when he perfected ground effects for F1. Andretti's 1978 championship-winning Lotus 79 was a gorgeous piece of work, and also an important trendsetter, a true landmark design. Yet to me this car was a bit too clinical to love. Nor did it stay competitive like earlier Chapman models. By 1979, the 79 was struggling. So was the marque, and it would never really recover.

No, in this 50th year of Lotus, it's still the fabulous 72 that's number 1 for me.

27

Maserati *Rinascita*

Vintage Racecar, February 2005

Mr. Cozza lifted the right side of the center-hinged bonnet and bent over the long, bristling racing engine. His colleague, Mr. Torbelli, flipped switches in the stark open cockpit. There was a complexity of mechanical grunting noises, then a sudden, staccato burst of machine-gun fire. *Sixteen cylinders* raucously voicing their *gioia di vita*.

Through oil-smoke rising from the headers I saw Cozza's leathered face break into a radiant grin. To me that said it all about Maserati's *rinascita*, the renaissance this once nearly moribund Italian automaker is enjoying today.

I'm glad to see it. During my impressionable youth, Maserati was one of the greatest marques in motorsports. The Trident on the noses of its cars proudly pierced finish lines in sports car and F1 races around the world, even twice at Indianapolis.

So many Masers I saw while growing up were so pleasing to my eye: the graceful two-liter A6GCS, the beautiful 300S, the boldly distinctive Birdcages. Of course, one of my—and everyone's—indelible images is of our great hero, Juan Manuel Fangio, four-wheel-drifting that loveliest of all Grand Prix machines, the 250F, to his final world championship in 1957.

Maserati may never have attained quite the stature of Ferrari, but did play a rich and vital role in the sport for a very long time. Then the

brand faded, not quite away, but into obscurity. Financial instability drove the venerable firm into the hands of one foreign entity after another, each seeming less and less to understand the value of what it had acquired.

The Trident owes its rebirth to Fiat, which now controls both Maserati and Ferrari and has placed both under the same kind of modern, energetic, and well-funded management. New and satisfying Maserati road cars are coming out of the old brick-walled factory in Modena, but better yet, Maserati is back in racing. Its MC12 supercar, derived from Ferrari's fabulous Enzo, closed the 2004 season with a couple of victories in FIA sports car events in Europe and Asia. Soon we hope to see it at Le Mans and perhaps in the American Le Mans Series.

Permit me once again to cheer an automaker that appreciates the importance of motorsports in building its image, corporate spirit, and technological expertise.

All this came together for me in September, when a US publication sent me on a junket to Italy in celebration of Maserati's 90th birthday.

Doing my homework in advance, for once, I read up on the grand history of the marque Maserati: how in 1914 several brothers of that name opened a tuning and race prep shop; how they took as their corporate emblem the three-pronged fishing spear held by the Roman god Neptune in a statue at the heart of their native Bologna; how they built the first car actually named Maserati in 1926, and promptly won their class in that year's Targa Florio.

For the next 10 years and more the Maserati brothers played right at the top of European racing, building a series of sports, GP, and speed record cars. This was the halcyon period that produced the 16-cylinder wonder I encountered in September.

That happened in the pit lane at the Mugello circuit, where it and more than 100 other historic Maseratis were making a track-day stop during a celebratory tour from the factory in Modena down to Rome. Though there was plenty else to look at, this wire-wheeled old warrior was obviously something exceptional. It drew our small party of journalists like a flame.

Mr. Cozza told us he is a lifelong Maserati man who joined the company in 1951, when he was 16, and who now works in its records department. He explained that the car we see today is mostly a recreation, though the engine and gearbox are original. That eye-filling engine is actually two in one, a pair of supercharged straight-eights mounted side by side on a common crankcase with the two crankshafts geared together. That means one rotates "backwards," and in keeping, its twin-cam cylinder head is a mirror image of the other, so all exhaust ports are on the outside.

To make room for the intake manifolds between the heads, the blocks are slightly canted outward. Maserati appropriately termed this a "V" configuration and added a numeral to indicate total displacement. Thus this 16-cylinder was a "V-4" when it first appeared at a displacement of just under four liters in 1929. That year it raced in the Italian Grand Prix at Monza, but earned its real distinction when

Baconin Borzacchini drove it along a 10-km course near Cremona to a speed record better than 154 mph.

The next summer the V-4 won a GP at Tripoli and was holding fourth at Monaco when it retired. Maserati even brought the car to the 1930 Indy 500, but as the rules there made it run without its superchargers, it performed poorly and retired early with ignition trouble.

Still, Maserati was encouraged by its monster's potential and increased both bore and stroke to create a "V-5." During the 1932 GP season the five-liter 16 showed up fairly well against Alfa Romeo's elegant new 2.6-liter straight-eight single-seater, despite the Maserati carrying more weight and having more frontal area due to its wide radiator and old-fashioned passenger seat. Unhappily, a crash in another speed record attempt that year killed its driver, Amedeo Ruggeri.

Rebuilt, the V-5 crashed again in the 1934 Tripoli race; driver Piero Taruffi survived, but the wreckage was put away and all but forgotten for the next 70 years. The restoration wasn't quite finished at Mugello, but the car did turn laps and sounded glorious.

In today's golden age of restoration we are seeing many fine old vehicles brought back from the dead, but it's something special when it happens in concert with the resurrection of the car's manufacturer. *Meraviglioso!*

28

Mercedes' Milestone

Vintage Racecar, March 2003

SHE WAS BORN to race, but was more amiable to drive than I'd expected, more like a production sports car with sharpened edges than a raw racer. Yet as a racer she was a real one. Mercedes-Benz 300 SL chassis 05 is a sister of the silver bullet that won Le Mans in 1952 and the actual second-place finisher from that year's Mexican Road Race.

Mercedes-Benz allowed me only a few miles behind the big, four-spoked steering wheel of this precious vehicle, one of the very ones that brought the company back to racing honor after World War II, but that was enough to confirm a sentiment I've been nursing almost since this lovely gullwing coupe was new:

Dammit, it's *right* for there to be a close family relationship between race cars and sports cars.

My hands-on experience with Mercedes' milestone machine came in Mexico last November, 50 years to the week after the venerable automaker scored its historic one-two finish in La Carrera Panamericana.

Nearly 2,000 miles long, that open road-race up the wild, mountainous Mexican interior was twice the length of Italy's Mille Miglia, and maybe several times as hazardous. It took five days to run, giddy days filled with the kind of misadventure and daring-do that create immortal legends.

Mercedes came to Mexico as a first-timer, probably not fully understanding the magnitude of the challenge. Certainly its tires were unsuitable, and all three race entries were plagued with tread separations. Inevitably, too, they ran into things, including a vulture that knocked a riding mechanic senseless. That crew's car finished the race wearing the famous buzzard bars on its windshield.

Yet it finished first. That might have been luck, but when another 300SL ("mine") placed second, pushing back to third the sole surviving Ferrari of a trio specially built for this race, it was obvious Mercedes had brought something more than luck.

That would be the renowned organizational ability of team manager Alfred Neubauer, the skill and determination of the technical staff under engineer Rudi Uhlenhaut, and the driving talent of winner Karl Kling, runner-up Hermann Lang and their new American team mate, John Fitch (who crossed the line fourth, but was disqualified for working on the car at an unauthorized location).

I think, also, that some of the 300 SL racer's strength in Mexico and also at Le Mans might have been that it wasn't a pure racer.

M-B had built plenty of those in the 1930s, and would do so again in 1954–'55, but the 300 SL of 1952 was essentially a high-level hot-rod. Uhlenhaut and the team had to treat their W194 project that way simply to get it built at a time the company was still recovering from

war. Thus, inside the sleek aluminum bodywork and state-of-the-art space-frame chassis was a relatively mundane engine, driveline and suspension package lifted from Mercedes' three-liter sedan.

True, both head and block of the SOHC, inline-six engine were specially cast for this application, and it was tilted to one side to lower the CG and hood line. Other detail modifications abounded elsewhere, but none of the mechanical parts punctured the envelope of the factory's production car experience. The racer was as reliable as a street car because, basically, it was one.

It sure drives like that. The experience begins with lifting the distinctive top-hinged door and clambering over the high, wide sill. Both design features, of course, accommodate the deep space-frame, which in fact is the car's only exotic element.

To let your legs in, this steering wheel comes off the hub (the hub was hinged in later production models). Once settled into the deep bucket seat, you notice an interior as nicely finished as in any fine 1950s sports car, with carpeting, chrome-trimmed gauges and switchgear that functions with smooth precision.

The carbureted engine fires readily but idles a bit erratically, as any hopped-up street car's would. The clutch is stiff but no bear trap, while the four-speed box under its long cranked lever feels much like any other car's of the era.

Given 170-odd horsepower and a dry weight just under 2000 pounds, acceleration isn't spectacular, but it's entertaining, the engine growling ferociously like a puppy with a pull-toy. I didn't notice any real steps in the power curve, just a sense the engine was happier the faster it spun. The 6000-rpm limit seemed too low, though I exercised discipline.

What everyone knows about the 300 SL gullwing coupe is that its swing-axle rear suspension made the car "a wicked and vicious final-oversteering monster," in the words of contemporary journalist Denis Jenkinson. I didn't attempt to feel this for myself; I've done so often enough in other swing-axle vehicles to believe Jenks.

What I can report is a delightful sense of direct honesty in 05's non-powered steering. Yes, it did call for a bit of muscle, and this particular steering box seemed worn and sticky, but the way the big wooden rim "talked" to my hands made me want to just take off, drive on through those gorgeous Mexican mountains for, oh, 2,000 miles or so.

They've perfected that feel of driving out of so many cars today. Most people seem to count ease of parking as more important. Even today's very high-performance road cars, such as the Mercedes-Benz SL500 and its tuned-up AMG55 variant, both of which I also drove on this trip to Mexico, interpose layers of numbing insulation between driver and road. Those models, in particular, have impressive technology to keep the wheels in line, and you can charge corners at incredible speeds with astounding stability.

But to me, such technology comes across like mama is along on the date. The leash grows irksome.

I think many racing fans—and I hope some racing drivers—feel the same about the computerized controls that have crept into today's race cars. I believe the unmasked, warts-and-all innocence is one big reason so many of us love vintage race cars.

There's no going back, I suppose, but I long for the era recalled by the 300 SL, a time when it was up to a driver to control his own damn traction, and when today's race car really could be tomorrow's sports car. *My* sports car!

29

Pedro and the 917

Vintage Racecar, April 2001

SOMETIME IN THE RAINY wee hours of the recent Rolex 24 at Daytona, a race I find myself covering again after a lapse of, gosh, decades, one of my younger colleagues turned and asked, "So what do you think?"

My response wasn't prepared, but it was instant. "Well, it's not Pedro and the 917."

I cherish such impromptu exchanges that ignite a whole rocket-ride of thought. Weeks later, I'm still mulling over what my subconscious was talking about. To help, I pulled out the Daytona reports published by *Autosport,* the English weekly, in 1970 and 1971, the years Porsche won with its 917K flat-12 coupe. What I relearned about the '71 race in particular made for an illuminating 30-year comparison.

One thing I relearned is, the written word is so much sharper than memories. I would have sworn I'd typed out both stories, but it says here I was just the photographer the first year; I didn't do both words and pix there until '71.

On the other hand, I hadn't remembered that Pedro Rodriguez was one of the winning 917 drivers on both occasions. Clearly, though, that driver-car combination burned an indelible track in my underbrain.

You must know about the Rodriguez brothers, those blazing meteors from Mexico. As fast as they were wealthy—which isn't always

the case, as you also know—they got into very good equipment very young, and quickly drove to the top.

Too quickly? Ricardo, the younger by two years, became a Ferrari F1 driver in 1961 at the age of 19. A year later, having driven only five Grands Prix, he died in practice for his sixth, trying to set fast time at his hometown event.

Pedro, the elder, seemed the more self-controlled. Born in 1940, he didn't move into F1 until 1963. Driving Lotus, Ferrari, Cooper, and BRM cars, he ran 55 career GPs, winning two. When I saw him at Daytona in January of '71, he had just turned 31 and was heading into his ninth F1 season. His last, sadly. He was to die in a Ferrari sports car in July.

He was racing sports cars because in those days it was normal for F1 stars to contribute their talents to other kinds of racing. And Pedro Rodriguez in a Porsche 917 was a talent to take your breath away. One of Denis Jenkinson's epic race reports, for me, was his description of Pedro hurling this big, powerful, notoriously difficult machine around a rain-soaked Brands Hatch. I remember arriving at the last word and noticing my breath coming fast.

Other Pedro stories involve his equally spectacular teammate from Switzerland, Jo "Seppi" Siffert. Porsche's factory effort was operated by John Wyer's JW Automotive. Wyer, a wonderful, towering presence known as "Death Ray," was a strict disciplinarian. But he couldn't prevent Pedro and Seppi from gleefully rubbing black tire marks into each other's baby-blue, 200-mph supercoupes.

At Daytona in '71, Rodriguez's driving inspired me to write this: "The last hour of Thursday practice was quite a spectacle. Pedro *really* tried, fishtailing wildly out of the corners onto the banking, nearly brushing the concrete wall, getting smoky wheelspin all the way up to the gear change, which was done on the rev limiter; all completely terrifying."

That wasn't quite good enough for pole against Mark Donohue's faster Ferrari 512M, entered by Penske. But at the start of the race, I continued, "Pedro grabbed up the challenge, switching his lights on defiantly. In five laps Pedro was flashing his lamps directly into Mark's mirrors, and in another lap he was feinting to pass. The Ferrari began departing from its ideal line at strategic points, and the two little wedges of color were nose to tail around the entire speedway."

Rodriguez finally did scratch his way to the front, outbraking Donohue around the outside into Turn 1. At the end of that sprint through the infield, I wrote that when the manx-tailed 917 fired back out onto the banking, "there could not have been room between it and the wall for an extra coat of paint."

A long evening, a long, long night, and a weary morning later, the Penske Ferrari had lost an hour after a midnight crash, and the Porsche was cruising along alone, something more than 40 laps to the good. That's when a gear seized on a shaft.

Changing the gearbox itself, so commonplace now, was not allowed then, so the JW mechanics had to laboriously pull out its red-hot internals and replace everything with parts from a spare transaxle. It took over an hour. By that time another Ferrari, a NART entry, had gone by into the lead, and the repaired Penske car was looming up close.

". . . the Porsche shot out of the pit in true Rodriguez fashion. [No pit road speed limits, either.] The engine was cold, the brakes were cold, the tyres were cold, the oil was cold, but Pedro was hot: his standing lap was 1:49.5!" Six seconds off his qualifying time, but evidently I was impressed. He won by a lap.

Also evident, from my supercilious "It's not Pedro . . ." remark, is that the spectacular performance I witnessed 30 years ago colored my perception of the 2001 race. Justifiably?

One of the shortcomings I perceived in this year's event was a dearth of factory cars. Daytona now is the opening round of the new Grand-Am series, a NASCAR affiliate structured for privateers. Not one of the Sports Racing Prototypes this year was entered by a big, famous automaker.

Well . . . back in 1971, I complained that not a single true factory team was present either, in that year's second round of the manufacturer's world championship.

This year, I noted, there were only 15 SRPs at Daytona, half a dozen fewer than last time.

However, 30 years ago I pointed out that the grid held but 10 of the headliner Group 5 cars, only three of which were front runners.

What about the state-of-the-art aspect? A disdainful quip going around Daytona this year poked fun at the "modern vintage" nature of the Grand-Ams, some of which, the fastest, are five and more years old in basic design.

But to be fair, by 1971 the Porsche 917 was a three-year-old, and the Ferrari 512 was two. Nobody was building newer Group 5s because the class was about to end.

Performance? The legendary 12-cylinder FIA coupes of 1971 could boast more 600 horsepower and top 200 on the Daytona bankings. Today's Grand-Am roadsters have about the same power—from a much wider variety of technologies—and are held down to the 180-mph range only by their high-downforce aero packages, which benefits them in lap speeds as a whole (circuit alterations since 1971 make direct comparisons futile.)

OK, but in the good old days didn't we get to see F1 drivers throwing sports cars around? Yes, we did, but drivers in these good new days aren't so shabby either. The '01 field held several former F1 drivers, and one, the fiery Allan McNish, is on his way back to F1. He forced his screaming Ferrari 333 SP to fastest race lap.

As for the wheel-to-wheel dicing that I wrote so much about in 1971, well, if magazines today allowed me as much space as *Autosport* did then (and if I could summon the same youthful stamina at the keyboard), I could have written reams about McNish vs. series champ James Weaver in a Riley & Scott Ford, plus many others.

Yes, things have changed. But not all for the worse. On reflection, I suspect that 30 years from now people will be nursing their own vivid memories of 2001. "Oh, Daytona '31 was OK," they'll be saying. "But it wasn't Allan and the 333 SP."

30

Scarab:
The Beauty of the Beast

Vintage Racecar, September 2002

SOME OF US—we know who we are—go all slack in the knees before certain racing machines. One example for me are the Reventlow Scarab sports cars of 1957-1958. They still rivet my eye over 44 years after I first saw their lovely lines.

Why? I am moved to wonder. We all love race cars, that's why we're meeting here today, but does every such vehicle ever made hold our eyes and our hearts in thrall? Not like the Scarab does, nor the F1 Gurney Eagle, the Maserati 250F, the Bugatti Type 35, some few others on mental lists we all keep. So what is that special magic power possessed by these icons?

In the case of the Scarabs, it's not only their graceful looks, not only their outstanding track performance, not only their impressive race record; it's their whole preposterous, unbelievable, fairy-tale true story.

Likely you know about Lance Reventlow and the racing organization he built, but ask yourself: if you were a Hollywood screenwriter, could you dream up a plot line anything like this? Here we have no run-of-the-mill wealthy young man, but "the richest baby in the world," the only son of the heiress to the Woolworth fortune,

Barbara Hutton, and a Danish Count named Kurt von Haugwitz-Reventlow. The union turned sour, leading to a sensational custody battle over the child that kept the press focused on him for life.

Though born in London in 1936, Lance considered himself thoroughly American and was living in the Hollywood Hills when he turned 21. Good-looking, personable and an enthusiastic race driver, he was everybody's idea of a millionaire playboy sportsman—on the outside.

Inside, he was made of better stuff. As so well-recounted in Preston Lerner's book, *Scarab* (Motorbooks, 1991), when the rich kid quietly announced he meant to build his own racing cars, his closest friends took him seriously. Bruce Kessler, himself a wealthy and successful California racer, and Stan Mullen, a Los Angeles attorney well known in sports car circles, helped Lance put together Reventlow Automobiles, Inc., in August, 1957.

They assembled a legendary team. First aboard was Warren Olson, veteran race mechanic and expert manager. He immediately went to the Kurtis Kraft shop and recruited a pair of craftsmen already known for their road racing specials—aluminum artist Dick Troutman and master welder Tom Barnes. Then he talked their favored driver—

Laguna Seca, 1958.

former paratrooper and dry lakes rodder Chuck Daigh—into becoming RAI's development tester and lead race driver.

Other names on that storybook crew that we still recognize today were Ken Miles, exercising his genius at specials-building to help design the Reventlow chassis; Phil Remington, an enduring legend in practical engineering; Jim Travers and Frank Coon, a.k.a. Traco, who tuned Reventlow's Chevys; Leo Goossen, famed for his Indy engine work, who would design RAI's later F1 engine, and the likes of body builder Emil Deidt, body painter Von Dutch, and a talented young body stylist named Chuck Pelly.

Together, this expert, purposeful and, yes, properly funded team created a brand new marque that would dominate US sports car racing and then bravely take on the world of Formula 1. A breathtakingly ambitious program. Breathtakingly American.

And it gleefully expressed Yankee irreverence. In polite society, Reventlow said he named his car "Scarab" after an ancient Egyptian symbol of immortality. Privately, he'd admit this reference to a dung beetle was his sly way of poking fun at those who invoked grander images for their cars.

But the humor was on the surface. Deep down, this was a serious young man on a personal mission. Tellingly, according to Lerner's account, it was Reventlow himself who insisted Daigh be driver number one, and treat the boss as number two. "You can't let me win unless I *can* win," Lance instructed Chuck.

Once, to a newspaperman, Reventlow explained, "I'm trying to escape the playboy curse. I want to prove I can do something other than inherit money."

I watched all this from afar, but with the wide eyes of youth. Mostly I read about the Scarabs romping all across America, but did get to see them do it once. It was at Laguna Seca. I remember a pair of hauntingly beautiful metallic blue shapes, noses held high, hurtling raucously out of a corner, nose to tail. Cars I had been raised to revere, such as Ferraris and Maseratis and Jaguars, dwindled behind, left in the Chevy fumes.

What strikes me in retrospect, especially, is that Reventlow's team accomplished all this within the context of its times. That is, Scarabs weren't new-tech. These cars embodied concepts that were traditional in the late 1950s: large-displacement engines mounted in front, tubular frames, de Dion rear axles, drum brakes, and bodywork hand-made of aluminum and shaped by the eye rather than the wind. These points also describe successful European cars of the era. Reventlow and his guys simply did the job better.

True, they missed catching the new wave of thinking sparked by Cooper's mid-engined cars. Hard to fault these California hot rodders for that—most European constructors also took a while to accept the new principles.

RAI did finally move toward mid engines, building a single second-generation Scarab sports racer, but by then Lance had lost interest. He'd done the two things he wanted: he'd shown the world he could build a top race team, and he'd determined his own level as a driver. His success at the first wasn't enough to outweigh his disappointment over the second. So he turned his back on racing.

Augie Pabst's Scarab posed at the Pabst home, ca. 1996.

This was a letdown to the rest of us, but it didn't diminish the stature of his victorious Scarabs, that mere trio of original front-engined sports cars that literally stamped their shape on an era.

And what a beautiful shape. We'd remember and honor these cars and their accomplishments even if they didn't so please our eye, but their sinewy, predatory poise secures their place in our hearts. Mine, anyway.

Rodriguez awaits his turn at Daytona, 1971.

Section 3

Events

31

Sebring:
Music of the Night

Vintage Racecar, May 1999

GOOD THING IT still lasts 12 hours, because it took me that long to hear the voice of the old Sebring. I had to walk to a remote spot and wait alone in the night before it finally spoke to me.

When I was assigned to cover this year's venerable enduro, I realized it had been 27 years since my last one. That's quite a span of time, a quarter of the whole history of auto racing and over half of my own chronology. Time enough for so much to change in the track and its surroundings, even in the way the event is conducted, that at first I felt like some racing Rip Van Winkle.

Happily, I found relief in tramping around the battered old airport course and identifying a few places that are still older than I.

Well, not really. In fact the Army's Hendricks Field, built on the isolated flats of central Florida to train B-17 bomber crews, dates to 1941. I was already a year old. But provincial little Sebring took up its giddy affair with the suave international sports car set in 1950. My own first fling still lay ahead. Grasping this straw lets me think I'm younger than the race.

When was your first Sebring? Some of us old-timers were asking each other that, and I claimed geezer points by saying 1952. But it

Penske's Donohue/Hobbs Ferrari 512M at Sebring, 1971.

was a guess, and on coming home I found it incorrect. In photo files left by my father, Ozzie, his earliest Sebring pictures are of the '53 race, won by Fitch and Walters for Cunningham. Though I don't have any recollection of being there, I might have been. Sebring used to be the Lyons family's annual excuse to get away from the New York winter.

In '54, Ozzie was in place at the U-bend before the pits to record Taruffi's valiant but vain effort in pushing his Lancia to the finish line, only to be disqualified for it. He and Manzon had been leading in the last hour when the engine broke, letting the Moss/Lloyd OSCA come by to its famous upset win.

My personal memories start in '56, when Ferrari won with Fangio and Castellotti. I wasn't driving alone yet, but I was getting interested, and watching that lithe, red-painted little Monza with its prettily pouting lips dancing to victory had much to do with fixing in my mind the image of the ideal racing car.

Don't you think Sebring itself played that role for many of us? When Alec Ulmann and friends set up the first race here on New Year's Eve, 1950, they were pioneers. Watkins Glen had been going only two years, and there wasn't much else in this country to suit the emerging tastes of sports car enthusiasts.

Suddenly there was Sebring. The annual Grand Prix of Endurance planted big-time international racing seeds on this continent exactly when our soil was most fertile. Can we remember, today, the excitement of learning that fabled foreign marques such as Aston Martin, Ferrari, Jaguar, Maserati, Porsche, were battling America's own gallant Cunningham on American ground to write world automotive history? Now the incredible cars and fascinating stars we had only seen in fuzzy pictures were right here, alive in our eyes, our ears, our nostrils. We could run our fingers along their fenders, if we dared, or shake their hands.

My mom, Gerry, still rolls her eyes and puts a lilt in her voice when she talks about meeting the notorious playboy Porfirio Rubirosa here (he co-drove a Lancia to second place in '54).

More than a race, Sebring was a place of escape for racers and race fans—and their families—from every chilly latitude to a sun-drenched week of palm fronds and Ferraris. It was a magical mixture: the aromas of orange blossoms and Castrol R, clear skies and clarion exhaust notes, exotic shapes of native birds and imported car bodies and beautiful people to be seen everywhere. That fiery European temptress, sports car racing, found Americans easy prey at Sebring.

Yes, there was grime along with the glamour, but that was a heady blend to us. Yes, the track was rough, but so were roads of the day, and the concrete slabs of old airports commonly hosted sports car races. Yes, for most fans it was a long way to go, but it was worth it. Sebring may have been no beauty, but it was a place of beauty.

While 1956 was the first Sebring I remember attending, 1966 was the first I covered as a photojournalist. Like Ozzie with Taruffi, I watched Gurney pushing his Ford around the U-bend to disqualification. Later that night, I stood at the tailgate of my Volvo wagon with black bag and chemical tanks, nervously trying to remember everything my dad had taught me about processing film by feel. It worked, and my pictures duly appeared in England's *Autosport*. Oh, the elation.

After the '72 race I went off after other kinds of racing. While I didn't forget old Sebring, I did forget about it. Going back after all this time was guaranteed to be a strange experience.

Walking around the entire circuit as I used to ("No one does that now!" scolded one of my Brit friends), I located only four short lengths of track remaining from "my day." The rest has been bypassed, built on, paved over. It was disorienting, and initially disappointing. My first attempt to watch brake discs and exhaust flames at night ended in frustration at a cement barrier.

Ah, but then I found my way to the back straight behind the pits, and satisfied myself that Sebring still offers an experience unique in American road racing.

Though not as long as it used to be, this is still 3100 feet of straight-line speed where even the fastest cars give a good 12 seconds of full-honk. What makes this site special is the darkness coupled with relative quiet, because isolation and obstructions block out disturbances from other parts of the course.

A fan who sneaks past the fence here can stand alone in the night, drinking in pure noise as the black shapes bullet by. Roaring, screaming, howling, singing, their 12s and eights and sixes and rotaries combine in infinite combination, the sound waves interfering or reinforcing one another in intricate patterns atop the bass notes, a crazed concerto without name or counterpart.

The magic of Sebring still lives.

32

Goodwood Revival:
The Sound of England

Vintage Racecar, November 1999

SATURDAY EVENING AT Goodwood's Revival. The light is fading fast under a heavy English overcast. The pasture grass of the remote car park is still wet from earlier rains. I trudge to my borrowed "saloon," tired after a long race track day—happy but tired. My only thought: is there enough in the well to make The Party?

I whirl at the sound of a Merlin. Leaping from the airstrip in the middle of the Motor Circuit comes a P-51 Mustang. Its long yellow nose bright against the gloom, its deep Rolls-Royce roar seeming to bounce from the leaden clouds, it slants close above my head and banks steeply back for a "beat-up" of the little aerodrome. As the predatory thing builds speed in the dive, it begins to scream.

I stand rooted to the soil. *This!* I think. This is how it *was!*

Before Goodwood ever became a race course, it was RAF Westhampnett. During the Battle of Britain, Spitfires and Hurricanes flew from here. Later, so did Anglo-powered American Mustangs. Over half a century on, the Earl of March has invited these wondrous old warplanes back to the Goodwood Revival, his riveting reconstruction of motor racing as it used to be.

At intervals during the day, one or more fighters lift off for sweeping, lilting aerobatic displays. They knife up into the clouds, cut down behind trees, slice back out low over the crowd like 300-knot scythes. No FAA clearance regulations here!

The snarl from the sky always stops conversations; ones I'm in, anyway. At one point that day, one of my local friends looked up with light in his eyes. "Ah, just listen to that," he said. "The sound of England."

As the race biz grows ever more globalized, homogenized, perhaps we sometimes forget the towering importance to our sport of this relatively miniature island nation. Yes, other peoples have great racing histories too, but isn't there a certain broadsword spirit that defines the British way? A particularly bright edge of combative ingenuity backed by dogged ferocity?

I think so, and I think the sword was forged and honed in such desperate fights for national survival as the war in their home skies. To the Brits, I believe, racing is a glorious continuation of their Battle for Britain.

I'm not sure I realized all this until that P-51 lifted my scalp, but the next day, the last of the Revival, I put more thought into what I was seeing.

For instance, the supercharged V-16 BRM. Usually these rare, extraordinary machines are seen only in quiet repose at Donington or Beaulieu (I made pilgrimages to both great museums this time), but Goodwood brings them to life. And what a tale of audacity their raucous voices tell!

Here is an instrument of war—no less—crafted in concert by 350 companies, formally backed by their nation, and designed by engineers who had spent more than a decade under assault both on the track and in the air from frighteningly advanced technologies underwritten by a hostile, ruthless government. The British Racing Green BRM was bloodied Britain's answer, albeit delayed, to the Nazi Silver Arrows.

Never mind that the immensely complex, overwhelmingly ambitious project ultimately failed. That it was tackled at all, especially at the time and in the circumstances, makes British Racing Motors one of the epic marques.

In a similar but opposite way, I was thrilled to see hordes of little F3s beetling around the 2.4-mile road course. They meant something special to me personally. Once, as a small boy, I was allowed to climb into one at Bridgehampton. I vividly recall thinking, "This is my size. I could handle this."

Others thought the same, and that's why these odd little open-wheelers are historically significant. In the same postwar years when BRM was striving for the summit of race car design, Cooper and other "blacksmith" builders were dropping half-liter motorcycle singles into crude tube frames. They meant only to give the common man access to a traditionally elitist sport. Unwittingly, they laid the foundation of today's Grand Prix racing.

Those two trains of creative thought came together, it seems to me, in the so elegantly simple Lotus 49. I remember being entranced by the pure logic of this stressed-engine confection in 1967, and the three racing at Goodwood—three!—rekindled my admiration. As does any work of art, Chapman's fine chassis and Duckworth's superb Cosworth V-8 appear to have sprung whole from a few deft strokes of a draftsman's pen.

That weekend I saw and studied many other splendid vehicles. Especially ones I seldom, if ever, see anywhere else: Altas, Connaughts, ERAs, Frazer-Nashes, HWMs. The Ferrari "Thin Wall Special." A Tojeiro-Jaguar. Three Cooper-Bristols. *Seven* GTO Ferraris. *Eight* Lister "Knobblies."

By my own reckoning, about 270 cars and 20 bikes took the green flag in 13 races. There were scores of additional cars running demonstration or parade laps, and many more on static exhibition. Not all were English, of course. France, Germany, Italy and the USA were well-represented. But, fittingly, England's racing history was the most richly presented.

As only the English can present it. Anyone who only knows North American vintage racing has no idea how hard the Brits drive! Just as their aerobatic pilots wring out their warbirds at the lowest possible altitudes, so their race cars are really raced. "That's what they're for," the drivers will declare firmly.

Their owners back them up. It's as though it would dishonor these machines to not show their full performance. If they get bent, and they do, well, they can be fixed. The country is full of craftsmen who live to do just that.

After all, the British have been forging weapons to defend their history for a thousand years. It's in the air.

33

Glamorous Racing Nights

Vintage Racecar, February 2000

ONE OF THE SIDE benefits of the race reporter trade is getting to hobnob with motor racing's glitterati at their glamorous soirees. Such as the evening I went to Stirling Moss's birthday party, where I stuck my camera lens into his cake.

It was my first Can-Am, at Bridgehampton in 1966. The recently retired driving legend was there for the series sponsor, Johnson Wax, and Saturday before the race was his birthday. Racers don't need excuses to party, but when they stumble onto a beaut like this they seize it.

Our press passes got my sister, Claire, and me into a very crowded, very dimly lit room. The crush of animated people backed us to a wall. I felt something smooshy. I glanced down. The Contax at my hip was slathered in creamy white frosting from a magnificent, many-layered cake reposing in state on a side-table. Mr. Moss's cake.

I departed as gracefully—and anonymously—as possible.

Ah, the old Can-Am. It's remembered for its great cars, and rightly so. With big powerplants and other unrestrained technologies, famous local and international drivers and mountains of American dollars, the Canadian-American Challenge Cup Series made road racing important on this continent. It was a time of dramatic, hectic change in society as well as in racing, and the wild old Can-Am perfectly

Jerry Schmitt whips up another delicious supper on the road to ... some race or other.

reflected this. Besides, the series provided me with a career, so all in all I remember it fondly.

Somehow, though, many of my best memories are of little things. Incidents that were incidental to history.

For instance, where in a formal account of the series itself would I find room to describe bathing in Gary Wilson's horse trough? Gary was a privateer Can-Am racer based outside El Dorado, Kansas. My buddy Jerry Schmitt and I stopped in at his ranch one cross-country day. A hot day. We'd been camping in my Econoline. It seemed the most natural thing in the world to refresh ourselves in this nice big galvanized steel basin full of cool, if slightly opaque, water. It was only when Donna Wilson appeared with her camera that we realized how odd we must have looked. I'd give a lot now to have that photo burned.

But I'd love to find a picture of the corral we set up in the parking lot of the Monterey Holiday Inn. Jerry lived in New Mexico, where he had horses, and one year we brought them along on the Can-Am's California swing. To ride on the beach, or something.

Where in upscale Monterey do you leave horses while you go off to the Laguna Seca auto race track? Simple. Jackknife van and horse trailer against the motel's back fence to form a triangular little corral, throw a couple flakes of hay over the top, and split for the day.

We spent three comfortable nights there in my van, showering in racers' rooms, and never heard a peep from the motel management. Monday morning we pulled out for Riverside, leaving nothing but a triangular brownish stain. I'm sure it washed right off in the first winter rain.

A downside of race reporting is that the best parties brew up after races. That's what I hear, anyway. I don't care to think of the number of Sunday evenings I've spent in gloomy track media centers or the false homeyness of motel rooms, trying not to listen to the distant din of revelry outside while tap-tapping away on my story.

Recently, while interviewing former McLaren manager Teddy Mayer about the old Can-Am days, I mentioned hearing that certain things went on after races. "Yeah, definitely," he said with a grin. "Quite a lot."

Maybe I got into the wrong end of the game, I mused aloud. Don't expect sympathy from a racer. "Could well be!" Teddy laughed.

This being a family-type publication, we won't continue down that road. But I can tell about sleeping in Denny Hulme's bed. Actually, I'd forgotten until he reminded me—and the world—during a Can-Am reunion banquet at Watkins Glen in 1990.

The genial old Bear stood at the lectern reminiscing, reminiscing, reminiscing, and I sat listening happily and taking notes until suddenly realizing: Denny was saying something about "this hippie who used knock on me motel door on Monday morning to have me carry his report to England, and when I'd gone he'd take a nice hot shower and snuggle into me nice warm bed for a snooze."

Not true! I was not a hippie.

However, in those distant days Before Computer you did indeed have to send paper and film to a magazine. England's *Autosport*, the newsweekly for whom I covered Can-Am and other events for ten years, needed material by Tuesday morning, London time. Mail wouldn't do it. Air freight was expensive, and carried risks of holdups in Customs. Best was to hand your parcel to a friendly racer heading home. Hulme was one who often obliged, and Stirling Moss was another. Until Texas 1969.

That was the season finale, and I really wanted to make Sunday night's party. Helped by Jerry Schmitt, who gathered postrace quotes while I pounded away on my manual typewriter in the J-Wax media trailer, I finished my story in record time, dashed with it to the College Station Ramada, and knocked on Stirling's door. "Right," he said, "leave it with me." At peace, I accompanied him downstairs to the party. It was a grand party. One of the few I ever made.

Weeks later, a copy of *Autosport* made its lengthy way to Jerry's home in Corrales. Eagerly, I turned to my story. But it wasn't my story. Not a word or picture did I recognize. And that byline . . . "Edgar J. Beaver" was clearly a British pseudonym.

I phoned London. Moss had forgotten my package, left it in the hotel, and with no way to contact me in those pre-cell phone days, my frantic editor scrambled to put something together on his own.

Several procedures changed after that, and one was to always make carbon copies. I hadn't done so that time, and the lost original has never surfaced. I still think it was the best story I ever wrote.

What I never asked Stirling was . . . had he found out about that birthday cake?

34

Monterey Historic Races:
Insights from Vendor Alley

Vintage Racecar, December 2003

SOME OF YOU MODEL makers, I know, and probably you historic artists as well, have been wondering why Jo Siffert's 1971 Can-Am Porsche, which normally was painted all dayglo-red, had blue trim on its nose for a couple of races mid-season. At long last I can tell you why.

That's because my wife, Lorna, and I undertook to spend the Monterey Historic weekend selling our photos and books from *Vintage Racecar Journal's* booth in Vendor Alley.

Though I agreed taking care of business is important, I secretly groaned. ("Not that secretly," Lorna is muttering.) I hated the idea of being locked away in tent city, out of the action, unable to see the race cars or talk with the racers.

What I didn't foresee was how many of the racers would come to the VRJ booth, and how much I would learn from—and enjoy—their visits.

"Hey . . . that's the *TREE!*" we heard a woman squeal. She was pointing at a picture hanging on the tent wall. I'd taken it here at Laguna Seca during the 1970 Trans-Am race. My wife, who has the people skills in the family, cozied over to the lady and inquired as to her interest in old-time Trans-Am cars.

"No, the tree! I've been looking all over for a picture of that *tree!*"

To me, the photo depicted two Pony Cars plunging down the Corkscrew. The frankly scraggly old oak was merely a compositional detail in the background. But to our excited guest it was an old friend.

Jane Newbury was a corner worker, she explained, and had been working that corner for, well, for a while. The tree used to shade the flag station at the crest of the hill, driver's left. "Then CART came along, and they said the tree was too close, it had to go," she related. "But the county wouldn't let 'em cut it down. So they moved it. Cost $16,000. And now it blocks our sight-line."

We were delighted to provide her a picture of how it used to be.

A man strode straight to a view of the starting grid of the Laguna Can-Am race in 1972, and tapped his finger on a blue McLaren positioned on row four right behind Denny Hulme. "That's my car."

Chuck McConnell was crew chief on that Mike Hiss-driven M8F that year, he continued, but he was also a Can-Am driver himself. Today he restores these grand machines. I was glad to talk with him.

And not half an hour later, a youngster came by and asked, "Do you get any race drivers coming in here?" Well, son . . .

Hey, we also got Tony Adamowicz. The champion in Trans-Am and F5000, Can-Am and Le Mans racer and founding member of the Polish Racing Drivers of America stopped for a nice chat. So did historic Can-Ammer George Drolsom. We also met David and Lorina McLaughlin of Europe's FORCE vintage series. I like their slogan: "History Not Victory." Other vintage racers to grace our booth included Brian Blain, John Delane, John Dimmer, and Dave Pozzi.

We even got David Hobbs. The jovial TV star said he was looking to find a photo of the GT40 he drove at Le Mans. I told him sorry, I wasn't there for that. "Well, if you ain't got anythin' of *me*, I'm leavin'!"

Someone else from the TV world dropped in, too. Apparently he knows our Publisher. Didn't catch his name, but he's got a rather notable jawline, and I hear he has a rather amazing collection of cars and motorcycles. Later I noticed him in the booth next door, shopping for a giant tool chest. The salesman was jumping up and down in a

Lorna and Pete at work at Monterey.

drawer to demonstrate how strong it was. "I'm not going to keep *people* in it," quipped the TV guy. I think he could make it as a comedian.

We met owners of historic cars, Lolas, McLarens, Tyrrells, even a Cunningham, who wanted pictures from historic times. Even more, they wanted to talk about those times.

"Our dad used to race a Porsche Speedster back East," brothers Asher and Dan Chapman told us, "and we used to sleep in George Weaver's barn at Thompson Speedway with his pre-war Maserati and all these great old posters, and we never thought anything about it."

Other visitors brought other stories, or observations, or questions. One introduced himself as model maker Gary Horrocks, reminded me we'd corresponded by email, and asked, "Did you ever find out why Siffert's Porsche had blue on its nose?"

Ah! I remember that puzzle. Another of my e-buddies, Joao Freitas in Portugal, also wants to know. Sorry, I had to tell Gary, I still had no idea.

The weekend went on. A big, muscular guy enfolded my wife in a bear hug. "I'm Bob West! Remember me from IMSA?" I caught up with an old friend of my own, Larry Roberts, who was art director at *Racecar* when I was editor. A gentleman who used to know my father said hello. One of my favorite editors came along and gave me another assignment, and a couple of fine writers presented me copies of their latest books. Legendary photographer Jesse Alexander took the trouble to look at my pictures and say polite things. So it was already a fabulous event for me, full of exactly those experiences I think we all enjoy about vintage racing, and then Edi Wyss appeared.

A master craftsman from Switzerland, Edi was Jo Siffert's mechanic in the 1971 Can-Am. He actually built that dayglo-red roadster from a pile of aluminum tubes in the Porsche factory, then shepherded it to a lucrative fourth-place finish in the points that season.

Siffert's Porsche. Edi Wyss. The penny dropped.

"Edi!" I exclaimed. "Why did you paint the nose blue halfway through the season?"

He smiled at the memories. He told the story. The little privateer team turned up at its first race, Watkins Glen, with the 917/10 finished in Porsche's standard, plain white. But Siffert, an energetic businessman, had cut a last-minute deal with STP. The night before the race a painter sent all the way from California sprayed on the company's trademark iridescent red, or "STPink," as we used to call it.

"Then the painter went home, and we went on to the next races," Edi continued. "When Seppi would hit something, we didn't have any more of the special paint, so I went to a store and found a shade of blue I thought looked nice with the red.

"When we arrived in Laguna Seca, the STP guy came back and painted the whole car again."

See why I love vintage races? So Gary, Joao, there's your answer.

35

Can-Am 1971:
The World's Fastest Ride

Vintage Racecar, October 2005

"A GREAT HAMMER struck my spine, slamming my head back. I forced it down, and stared at the long black roadway between the orange wheel bulges. It was rushing like some demonic torrent frantic to enter the gates of hell . . ..

"There was no longer any sensation of speed. We were going too fast."

I chose that quote from myself to start my book *"CAN-AM"* because, if we strip that glorious old Canadian-American Challenge Cup sports car series down to its naked essence, it was all about raw, wild speed—that, and the joyous fact the cockpits had room for nut cases like me to ride along in the midst of the maelstrom.

My rocket ride with Peter Revson came at Riverside in 1971, a few days before he clinched the driver's title, the first American to do so. The champion's car was his no. 7 McLaren M8F, a caramel-colored, fin-bedecked "Batmobile" weighing a claimed 1,520 pounds with 509 cubic inches of Reynolds Aluminum Chevy in the back. Power? Seven hundred-something; who really knows. It was a huge number in those days.

A number big enough to make Can-Ams the fastest road racers on

the planet. Whenever they and F1s visited the same tracks in the same year, the Big Bangers almost always set quicker laps than the delicate little single-seaters, which had two-thirds the power and probably half the torque. No, the sports cars weren't as nimble, not nearly, but they had the power to drag more downforce around the course, and thus could corner fast without giving up straightaway velocity.

And the McLaren M8F exemplified this. It was a wide "racer's wedge" (a term coined for an Indianapolis Lotus a few years earlier) with air-fences molded into the outer top surfaces of the bodywork (a Peter Bryant idea introduced on his Titanium Car two years earlier). These fences held high-pressure air atop the body, rather than allowing it to spill off to the sides, finally ducting it to the big rear wing between those rising fins. The shape's whole purpose was to harness airflow to stick the car to the road.

The principle was starkly contrasted by 1971's other main contender, the Lola T260 driven by Jackie Stewart. In those happy experimental days, when the laws of physics and the rules of the game seemed equally open, Lola took the opposite aerodynamic tack: to shape the car like a bullet and rely on the World Champion's talent to get it around the turns.

The T260 even started out with small-diameter front wheels, 13-inchers rather than the usual 15s, for lower frontal area. That idea didn't survive early testing, but in its first races the car still was all about straightaway velocity. Its nose was blunt, with just some air outlets on top and a small splitter around the bottom. The rear wing was tucked low over the engine cover, not hung out to the rear as on most cars, proving there wasn't much front-end downforce to counteract.

Stewart did his part and set some great lap times, even taking pole away from McLaren's Revson and Denny Hulme a couple of times, and managing two early season race wins when the two-car Kiwi juggernaut faltered. But the single-car Lola effort had failures of its own, often serious ones. The increasingly disgruntled Stewart—his mood not lightened by battles with myopic North American officials over track safety—saw that talent couldn't beat technology. He kept demanding more and more downforce so he could corner with the McLarens. By the end of the season, the "bullet" had been bewinged.

And what a wing: Lola hung an ungainly big airfoil way out ahead of that stubby nose like a snowplow. It looked ridiculous, and it didn't help much. The car never won again. At the end of the season Stewart signed to drive for McLaren in '72, though an ulcer would keep him from doing so.

Jackie never offered me a ride in the Lola. Having watched its antics, I'm not sure I'd have accepted. But I jumped at the chance to cram myself into Revson's McLaren.

Cram is the word. I was instructed to cross my ankles, the only way my shoeless feet would fit into the narrow left-side well. I was told to stretch my left arm way out across the wide metal monocoque (the car's total fuel capacity was *72 gallons!)* so I could hook my fingers over its outer edge. I would find out why a little later. Someone pulled my right hand up behind my head and ordered me to maintain a death grip on the roll bar. For one thing, none of us wanted my arm falling into Revvie's sphere of action. For another, my own sinews, such as they were, would be responsible for holding me in when the brakes went on.

What, no belts? Former McLaren mechanic Alec Greaves, now a tech inspector for historic Can-Am races, likes to claim he personally belted me in that day. I maintain there were no belts for that seat, because I vividly recall the sensation I'd pivot out over my heels if I didn't hang on tight. We really didn't worry about things like belts in those days. Not when given an opportunity like this.

I do believe him when he says that when Peter fired the Chevy, he gave Alec a wink. "I knew right then, mate, he was going to frighten you silly!"

Hah, not a prayer of that. Hadn't I read my Jenkinson-rides-with-Moss stories? Hadn't I long admired Peter Revson's smooth skill, and watched the cool competence of that series-winning M8F? Frightened? Me?

Well . . . there was the sight of Riverside's infamous boilerplate wall coming at us for the first time. Seen at speed from Riverside's mile-long back straight, the barrier around the right-hand Turn 9 looked like a steel gate to the Underworld.

What speed? When I last glanced at the tach it was swinging through 6,600 rpm, which later I worked out to be 184 mph. But we were still accelerating, and for some reason my gaze then locked onto that wall. So I can't prove it, but I'm sure we went up beyond 190.

Just before the wall the straight kinked to the left. At a Formula Ford pace it was quite a gentle kink. In a Can-Am car at 190 it took every ounce of strength I could will into my desperate fingers to hang onto that fuel tank. This is where I finally, fully understood the power of aerodynamic downforce. In slower turns, like 6 or 7, there hadn't been much side-force. Here, it was unreal.

And then, at last, the brakes. Revvie's leg made a single strong motion, and *UUUMMPHH*. We practically stopped. It was the turn of my right hand, up behind my helmet, to keep my poor, floppy rag doll of a self in place.

Mountains of dollars' worth of technology, and it still comes down to human flesh and nerve. That's what I learned about racing from that ride.

36

Targa Florio:
VV NINO!

Vintage Racecar, April 2006

SICILY'S WILD OLD Targa Florio rates as one of the most appealingly primitive speed events I've ever been to. Most race organizers strive to spread a frosting of civility over this nutty-fruitcake business, but they don't seem to worry about that in Baja, nor did I see much of it my one time at the Safari rally.

The Targa was equally untamed. Looking back on three trips there, my prime memories are things such as:

• The team who opened their rented garage on race morning to find their Porsche race car missing. In its place was a courteous note: the proprietor of the restaurant in which they'd dined the evening before—but had left without paying—had borrowed their *macchina* only temporarily, and would return it promptly at the end of the day.

• Mingling with all the other spectators along the wide-open race course, swinging our legs out from stone walls practically over the driver's helmets and strolling freely on the circuit itself until we heard the next car coming.

• Watching the racers come pounding down out of the mountains and sliding out onto the seaside straightaway, just about their only respite from the endless swerves and turns elsewhere around the 44-

mile circuit. And quite a respite it was: that straight was a glorious four flat-out miles long. You could hear the 12-cylinder Alfas and Ferraris winding away through all the gears and then holding peak revs in fifth for a long, long time, until their dwindling note finally was lost in the song of twittering birds in the olive and lemon trees. Now that was magic.

Having grown up on stories about open-road races like this, and keenly aware it was the last one left by the time I was old enough to go, I tackled my first Targa trip in 1962. I went by motorcycle, a single-cylinder, 350cc Norton I'd bought second-hand in England. Sicily was a long way from there, a long, delicious way down through France and the Maritime Alps to Monaco, then on down the entire gorgeous, hilly length of the Italian boot into ever-warmer springtime weather of the Med.

One night down there in the peninsula's toe, as was my custom, I maneuvered the bike into a convenient grassy field and was unrolling my sleeping bag when I heard a challenge in the darkness. I could just make out the farmer's silhouette against the fading sky light. "*Buona sera,*" I greeted him in my best bogus Italian, and tried to explain that I was a weary traveler in his lovely land, and hoped very much he would not mind my passing a peaceful night here in his fragrant and doubtless fertile field.

His response was terse: Get on your "*moto*" and "*partita.*" Hmm, I thought, I need to make friendly, face-to-face contact. I stepped forward to plead my case.

In silhouette I saw both his elbows snap up. Shotgun. I couldn't see it, but I sure could sense it pointing at my chest. So I got on my *moto* and *partita'd.*

From then on I chose my campsites with more care. One night, having finally reached Sicily, I stopped at a small police station and was able to secure permission to sleep on their lawn.

Sicilians, I found, look gruff and stoic and unapproachable until you do approach them, then they become as friendly as Brazilians. I remember stopping the bike in a cobblestoned village square to study my map, and suddenly being aware I was surrounded. A dozen

The winning Merzario/Munari Ferrari 312PB cornering at Collessano, Targa Florio, 1972.

lean, sun-burnt men were gazing at me with rigidly impassive faces. I suddenly perceived how alien an apparition the helmeted me on my uncommonly large motorcycle must have been in this ancient mountain town so remote from the tourist paths of central Europe. Were they thinking of . . . shotguns?

Nervously, I cracked a smile.

Instantly, every face ringing me burst into a warm smile and animated fingers began offering friendly route guidance. Everybody wanted to know all about my Norton, and my declaration of its displacement, "*Tre cento cinquanta,*" brought respectful awe. By the time I motored away, I felt embraced like family.

Finding the famous *Piccolo Madonie* circuit turned out to be no problem; it was clearly marked by the "VV NINO" signs hand-painted on about every second stone wall. Race driver Nino Vaccarella was a Sicilian native, and I gather "VV" signified a universal sentiment that he have a good long life, or at least win the race. (He would—three times.)

179

Watching the Targa Florio race was not the same as following it. Perched somewhere along the long, long course, your Italian not really good enough to grasp the excited commentary coming over the occasional portable radio among the crowd, you really couldn't be sure who was leading and by how much.

But it was enough to soak it all in: the sun blessing the trees and flowers and red tile roofs; the gnarly old road winding up and down across the vast, craggy island vistas; the screams of racing engines rising, rising toward you and then the cars themselves bursting into sight, the drivers in a flail of fury, sliding, correcting, just missing roadside stones—or not—and hustling on away to their place in history.

I made it back twice more, in 1972 on another motorcycle and the following year in my brand-new Corvette, which I had ordered in bright Targa Red. Both expeditions were rich, indelible experiences.

I've honestly forgotten some races I've been to, but I'll never forget the Targa Florio. It was my idea of what racing is.

37

USAC Road Racing:
Leftists Turning Right

Vintage Racecar, January 2008

How AMUSING, I often smile, that a breed of racer I associate with conservatism generally speeds around to the left. But we don't do politics here, just history, so let's have a look back at interesting times when oval drivers first tried their hands at turning both ways.

The big ones for me were the three USAC Rex Mays 300-milers at Riverside, California, in 1967, '68 and '69.

You might remember USAC. Time was, the United States Auto Club stood as the grizzly bear of American racing. This group began as a replacement for the American Automobile Association, which long had been the sanctioning body for the Indy 500 and other major open-wheel events in this country. When AAA abruptly turned its back on the sport after the 1955 Le Mans disaster, Indy owner Tony Hulman created USAC.

Through most of the next quarter century, USAC remained the dominant force in U.S. professional motorsports, and not only on open wheels. Although NASCAR was growing in importance, USAC maintained its own stock car series. USAC also set up a pro sports car championship that attracted road racers scornful of SCCA's early ban on driving for money. Carroll Shelby won that USAC title in 1960, clinching it at Riverside with a Birdcage Maserati in his last-ever race.

But the Rex Mays events later that decade were part of USAC's mainstream Indy car series, its season finale, in fact. Just as today, back then road courses such as St. Jovite in Canada and Indianapolis Raceway park, and also the Pikes Peak hill climb, offered sites for USAC events where no suitable speedways existed. Good old Riverside International Raceway was nicely situated on the edge of the vast Los Angeles marketing basin.

Rex Mays had been a Riverside native, a highly-regarded AAA champion and four-time pole starter at the Indy 500. Thirty years prior to the race named for him he had driven an Alfa Romeo against European stars in the Vanderbilt Cup road race in New York.

Gurney, the Black Knight, during practice at Riverside, 1969.

Riverside's first Rex Mays race in '67 drew a worthy entry. Of course all the big Indy stars came, including Mario Andretti and A.J. Foyt, who were still dueling for that year's championship. Others of their speedway fellows included Al and Bobby Unser, Lloyd Ruby, Joe Leonard and Roger McCluskey. But master road racers Dan Gurney and Jerry Grant were there too, and so were F1 champions Jim Clark and John Surtees.

Gurney vs. Clark! One of the classic confrontations. Dan had prepared one of his new Eagles with one of his own engines, a stock-block, pushrod Ford displacing 5.0 liters. He qualified on pole. Jimmy started alongside, not driving a Lotus, for once, but a Vollsted powered by a 4.2-liter, four-cam Ford, the conventional Indy engine of the era.

From the rolling start Gurney charged away with Clark tight on his tail, piling on pressure until Dan made a slight mistake on braking and ran wide. Jimmy seized the lead, but then his many-valve Ford broke one and he was out. That left the stock-block Eagle with a comfortable lead, until Gurney made his mid-race refueling stop. A tire had to be replaced too, and that cost so much time Dan dropped to third behind new leader Andretti (Hawk) and Bobby Unser (Lola).

That's when the winner of that year's Belgian GP and Le Mans showed his real mastery of Riverside. Gurney was carving as much as 1.5 seconds a lap from Andretti's lead, but Mario was responding and Dan's challenge looked hopeless—until six laps from the end, when the leading car spluttered and veered in to refuel.

That left Unser just ahead of Gurney, and it stayed that way until the very last lap of the 116, when the Eagle flew by to win. Dan fans still reckon that was one of the best drives of his great career.

Defending USAC champion Andretti came back out third, but Foyt was still placed to take the title. Although A.J. had already crashed his original Coyote, driver swapping was allowed in those days and Foyt sprinted back to the pits to take over teammate Leonard's car.

Bad news: Leonard's Coyote-Ford had already blown up.

Good news: McCluskey realized the fix his friend (and fellow Goodyear-contracted driver) A.J. was in and came in from second place to hand over his Eagle. As he had been behind then-leader Gurney at the time, Roger might have been in line to win.

Foyt charged out in fifth place, and that would be enough to deny Firestone-contracted Andretti the title. Then Foyt's "new" car slowed with clutch trouble, and he fell to sixth behind Grant. Advantage Mario!

But then Grant dropped out! So Foyt finished fifth after all and was 1967 champion.

The 1968 Rex Mays 300 also was a championship decider, this time between Indy winner Bobby Unser and points leader Andretti. Mario actually raced three cars that November day. He led off by passing and repassing poleman Dan Gurney, but when his Hawk-Ford blew up Andretti jumped into Joe Leonard's AWD Lotus-P&W Turbine—a device he'd never driven. Maybe that's why he tangled with the identical car of Art Pollard.

Mario wound up in Lloyd Ruby's Mongoose to finish third for the second year in a row. That cost him the championship, as Unser came second again, but has anyone but Mario Andretti ever driven that many cars in one race?

Winner? Gurney, of course, and again in an Eagle with 5.0 Ford.

For 1969 Dan came with a special new weapon. The new Eagle was all sharp angles, rather than the previous svelte curves, and its trick engine was equally sharp. Now displacing 5.2 liters and running as much as 20 percent nitromethane in its methanol, it impressed its builder-driver by going faster on the straight than his seven-liter McLaren Can-Am car could. "It's got a lot of power, *lively* power," Gurney told me for my *Autosport* report. "I think its one of the toughest things I've ever tried to handle."

Looking like the Black Knight in his full-face helmet, Dan won pole by over a second from Mark Donohue (Lola-Chevrolet). But neither Gurney's appearance nor his reputation intimidated Donohue or Mario Andretti (Brawner Hawk-Ford), who started third. Both chased Dan hard and managed to slip into the lead at different times. But Andretti had to pit with a flat tire, and Donohue pulled in with a cracked head.

So Gurney was on form for his third Rex Mays victory in a row
. . . until with just minutes remaining the powerful Eagle snapped a
half shaft. He kept going, but slowly, and both Andretti and Al Unser
(Lola-Ford) scrambled by. For Mario, this eighth win of the year,
including Indy, capped his third USAC championship.

For 1970 the Indy-copy Ontario Motor Speedway opened nearby,
but closer to L.A., so those 900 memorable miles of the Rex Mays
era were over. But what a bright time it was. True, the crowds were
never what the promoter hoped for, but grids ran to 30 cars, cars wild
in both their performance and their diversity. Driving them, plus the
names mentioned we saw the likes of Brabham, Bucknum, Cannon,
Dallenbach, Follmer, Heimrath, Johncock, Malloy, Mosley, Posey,
Revson, Rutherford, Savage, Scott, Sessions, Titus, Vukovich . . ..

Why can't we have such grand spectacles today? Racing has gotten
too darn conservative.

38

Pikes Peak:
Racing into the Sky

Vintage Racecar, July 2011

I EDGED MY TOES to the brink of an abyss a thousand feet deep, issuing my own small dare to this mighty mountain, and from this precarious apex of the world I gazed a hundred miles out to the vast eastern horizon, where dawnlight was rising to join me in the icy sky.

As one does, I found a stone, flung it out and watched it vanish far, far below my boots. That drew my eyes down to where I could just make out eagles spiraling into their first sorties of the morning.

Far below them, I knew, hidden in the still-dark forest, hunters of another sort were stirring.

This May, we celebrate the centennial of America's oldest continuing auto race, the Indy 500. It's proper we do so, but let's reserve an appreciative thought for our *second* most venerable speed contest, one a scant five years younger but a cosmos apart in concept, kind and character.

It was August of 1916 when racers first tackled Pikes Peak. Rather than a 2.5-mile, paved speedway sprawling across flat Indiana farmland at about 750 feet of elevation, the Colorado course is 12.42 miles of rustic road writhing up the north face of one of America's loftiest summits—14,110 feet.

Where they start the race, on pine flats above the Crystal Creek Reservoir, the elevation is 9,390 feet. and air pressure is reduced to about 70 percent of sea level. Atop the barren, stony peak, lungs and engines alike gasp to pull in oxygen from atmosphere that has fallen to 61 percent of normal density.

Indy has four almost identical turns lined with walls. The "Race to the Clouds" presents drivers with 156 corners, all of which are different and outside of which are boulders, or trees, or . . . nothing.

On my first drive up there, way up there, I came to a stretch that had me cowering on the wrong side of the road, creeping along, hugging the cliff, anxiously keeping my timid wheels away from the yawning void to my right.

A couple years later I ventured up again. An old hand, right? Again, I felt my courage draining along with the oxygen.

Pikes Peak aces laugh at people like me. Bobby Unser, the all-time champion on this mountain, has a reputation for offering reconnaissance rides in his rental car to innocent first-timers, just out of courtesy, don't you know.

There's a particular left-hander called the Blue Sky Turn because that's all you see beyond the edge. Hammering uphill into this, at precisely the crucial instant, BU yells "NO BRAKES" and desperately cranks the steering hard over, but the car plows unabated to the brink and plunges . . . out onto the previously unseen broad gravel parking area beyond.

His passenger's panic appears to make Unser's day.

Real racers delight in dancing on edges, and can you name a race course edged with more potentially cataclysmic chasms than the Pikes Peak Hill Climb? Simply being there, watching, is a unique experience in all of motorsports, and that's true even for 13-time winner (10 overall) Bobby U.

He told me one day, "There's a place you can go, the Devil's Playground, where you can watch the cars coming up for miles and miles, turn after turn after turn, and you can hear the engines roarin' all the way. In the old days, before they started puttin' down the calcium chloride [and more recently, asphalt], the cars would really be slidin' around them turns, throwin' roostertails of rocks and dust out. There was nothin' prettier in this world. It'd give anybody goosebumps to see it."

Our conversation was in 1994, when Bobby was competing in a stock car class with a vintage Torino. That wasn't one of his successful years, but his son Robby, already a multiple winner, had a real chance to set an overall record. Only one man stood in his way: Rod Millen.

It was a battle of utter opposites. Young Unser's Open Wheel class vehicle was only a year old, but could trace its conceptual lineage way back to 1916. A tube frame single-seater built by Speedway Motorsports, it carried its normally-aspirated, 420-inch Chevy in the midship position and put a claimed 700-plus horsepower (presumably a sea level figure) through a Lola transaxle to its rear wheels only. Gigantic airfoils made downforce at both ends. Reported weight was under 1800 pounds.

Millen's Toyota was a new entry in the Unlimited class. At Pikes Peak, "unlimited" means exactly that. The rule book contains only one rule and it permits, in so many words, "any race vehicle that is capable of obtaining a new track record . . ." Period.

Better than Can-Am!

That incredibly free hand allowed Rod Millen Motorsports, Toyota Racing Development and body designer Lee Dykstra to draw up a sort of rally funnycar with an IMSA GTP motor. A 2.1-liter turbo-4 left over from Dan Gurney's Eagle P-car program, it nestled ahead of the closed cockpit and drove all four wheels through a Weismann transmission. Engine man Drino Miller told me "This engine would make 930 horsepower at sea level," meaning maybe 650 at the start line, but rumors put total weight at a porky 2550 pounds. A Celica lookalike, the fiberglass body had a wing only at the rear, but there were ground effects tunnels.

During qualifying, run on the first 5.5 miles of the course to Glen Cove, Unser's Open Wheeler was faster than Millen's Unlimited by six seconds. That was despite losing 19 mph through a straightaway speed trap, where the winged Chevy racer clocked 110 mph to the Toyota coupe's 129.

Unlimiteds race last, meaning Rod Millen had to wait for Robby Unser and the rest of the Open Wheelers to make their climbs. As at the Targa Florio or the old Nürburgring, one follows this race mostly on the radio. Roaming the summit with short steps, trying to breathe, I heard excitement building all over the mountain as 1993 winner and outright record holder Paul Donner made another great Open Wheel run, cutting 16 seconds off his previous best, blasting to the top in 10:27.24.

But Unser was right behind, and escorted by helicopters and shouting fans he powerslid over the finish line at a stunning 10:05.85!

Robby was being interviewed when Rod finally launched. He tore through the Picnic Area at 128 mph (Unser's speed had been 119). Up into Glen Cove, the 4x4 Celica rounded a certain curve at 96 (Unser, 95) and stormed the next straight at 117 (vs. 110). Zig-zagging up "The Ws" to the Devils Playground and on into the Bottomless Pit, clocking 121 on the downhill straight there . . ..

Only 121? Exactly the same speed as Unser.

Up the last steep slope to the summit, the final hairpin was fenced by people leaning into the road, wondering what could be wrong with the Toyota. Here it came, the low-slung, soap-shaped coupe shooting into sight, darting around the turn and thrusting away, all four tires clawing the road.

How different Millen's Unlimited looked from Unser's tall, winged Open Wheeler, whose naked front wheels had been waggling and its huge rear knobbies spraying gravel. How different the turbo-Toyota's dronings and whistlings and chirp-chirpings from the hearty, open-pipe roar of the big, beefy Chevy.

What would be the difference in times?

Less than 2 seconds!

And Millen was faster! Ten minutes, four-point-zero-six seconds! It was another new record!

Brakes, explained Millen, his faced wreathed in smiles. The road surface, so often iffy here, was good for once, so grippy he'd overheated the brakes. That's why he'd backed off early into the turns those last few miles, giving the pedal three pumps to get it up. But the car itself was *perfect*.

As for himself, he allowed, he had put in a 100 percent performance. Never put a wheel wrong, all 156 turns. "I'm very pleased."

Unser, meanwhile, was already in a helo, heading down. No need to ask what *he* was thinking. "Next year."

39

Spanish GP 1975:
The Barcelona Boycott

Vintage Racecar, May 2003

ONE SUNNY SPRING day in Spain, 23 Grand Prix drivers shut themselves into a van in a race paddock, refusing to come out and drive their F1 cars. The event promoters threatened to seize the cars and all other team assets. Tensions escalated almost to the pointing of guns. Tragically, the dispute became seared into history when the weekend closed with an unrelated fatal accident.

If you've ever wondered how Bernie Ecclestone assumed such power over the sport, come back with me to Barcelona in 1975 and witness the chaotic dearth of official control in those primitive days.

The lovely old Mediterranean city's Montjuich Park was a dramatic setting for a motor race. The 2.355-mile lap of park roads and urban avenues began atop a commanding hill, plunged steeply down through several hairpins and near-hairpins that curled around ornate stone monuments and wonderful Olde Europe buildings, then climbed back in a series of tingly-fast arcs with trees on every side and a wide view of the Mediterranean beyond. I thought it was a beautiful circuit, faster and more varied than Monaco.

Yes, it was a dangerous circuit, but weren't they all in those days. The cars were no better, mere canoes of folded aluminum. We typically lost one or two F1 drivers a year. That's why Jackie Stewart, in particular, had been crusading for safety improvements.

And in fact the Royal Automobile Club de Cataluna y Baleares had been among the first GP organizers to install steel guardrails around its entire track. Jochen Rindt thanked the club with a gold-plated piece of the very barrier that, he felt, had saved his life in his Montjuich accident of 1969.

But when drivers arrived in 1975, they found the guardrail installation grossly negligent. After several years of being taken down and put back up, the battered, mismatched lengths of aged steel had many bolt holes so enlarged that nuts couldn't be expected to hold without big washers or reinforcing plates. At numerous points there were no such reinforcements.

Worse, hundreds of nuts—someone claimed to have counted, and I tested some myself—had not been tightened, and on many bolts there were no nuts at all. Nor were the posts securely planted. The structure was so flimsy you could shake it with your hand.

The drivers balked. At that time most belonged to a group called the Grand Prix Drivers Association (GPDA), and from their strength-in-numbers they issued an ultimatum: the barriers must be put right, or they wouldn't drive.

Perhaps there was a moment when cool heads could have averted a crisis. The moment passed.

I first learned of the situation when I strolled into the paddock shortly before first practice on Thursday (they used to have a *lot* of practice in F1). The paddock had been set up in the roomy expanse of a sports stadium, which ought to have been filled with an orderly bustle as engines were warmed and tools conveyed to the pits.

But crewmen were lounging around in the Spanish sun, their shirts off. The chief mechanic to reigning World Champion Emerson Fittipaldi was sprawled on his back atop a sidepod of the number one McLaren M23, his eyes closed. He didn't bother to open them when I expressed my admiration for how well-prepared he seemed to be for a practice that was due to start in 15 minutes.

"No practice now, mate," Alister Caldwell responded comfortably. "We're not going out 'till four, and prob'ly not then."

I found Emerson. He described how disturbed he'd been when he arrived on Wednesday and seen how the barriers were being assembled. "But they told me always, 'Tomorrow, tomorrow.'"

In his and everyone's mind were the faces of friends—including Rindt, in 1970—who had died when steel guardrails split apart or leaned back on impact.

Ronnie Peterson expressed the GPDA feeling this way: "Before Watkins Glen last time we all knew the guardrail wasn't right, because of Francois' [Cevert] accident [in 1973]. We discussed it, but we decided to go ahead and race anyway, and Helmuth [Koinigg] was killed. Now we want to make a stand."

But, no surprise, the drivers weren't unanimous. Jacky Ickx was one who did not agree with the majority opinion. "I am not a member of the GPDA, and so I feel free to do what I think is the right thing," he explained to me. "We are here now, and we are here to race . . ..

"The minute you start to race, you are pushing everything to the limit. It cannot be made safe. Motor racing is dangerous. It's made like that."

So Ickx was one of three drivers who strapped into their cars and began screaming around the circuit. The sound was clearly audible to the 23 who had holed up in a bus-sized hospitality van, determined to resist all pressure to come out and drive.

And pressure there was. Some of it was simply the weight of public opinion. There were plenty of people who felt the drivers should stop being sissies and go do what they were paid to do. "We pay them a lot because they say it's dangerous," commented one team manager.

Of course the event promoters were applying pressure, so were team owners and managers, and evidently some drivers in the van were wavering. The sounds of rivals earning grid positions must have been making them restive. Rumors went around among those of us outside that Fittipaldi used some strong-arm to keep his fellows inside.

One party conspicuously not involved was the FIA, the purported governing body. Its trio of observing officials from the Sporting Commission (CSI) took the position they were on hand merely to see that the circuit met the letter of FIA rules, and in their view it did.

Their attitude infuriated the GPDA. Said acting association president Graham Hill, "... as we feel the CSI are not doing their job properly, and as it affects us, we're taking the matter on ourselves.

"We've tried to find them now, to give them our views," Graham added during a Thursday evening press conference, "but they've gone home."

"They don't care," spat a bitter Niki Lauda. "They've only made one mistake," put in a sardonic James Hunt, "and we got to talk to them once. The rest of the time they've very skillfully been at lunch, or changing for dinner ...."

The stand-off dragged on through Friday. That afternoon, circuit officials promised workmen would be on the job all night and the barriers would be right by Saturday noon. The drivers didn't believe it then, and they still didn't Saturday morning. Lauda came back from an inspection ride on a motorcycle and reported tersely, "It's the same as yesterday." Hunt, seated behind him, said, "They've done some work, but it's cosmetic."

At 10 minutes to noon a cluster of team personnel broke up and some of them began sprinting to their transporters. What's up, I asked. "We're going to try to get the organizers to let us do two hours' worth of work on the guardrails ourselves," John Surtees answered. "Let's do it anyway," I heard Ken Tyrrell say.

And so for two hours, the time remaining until the 2 p.m. practice, there were men wearing colorful F1 team garb out around the Barcelona circuit with toolboxes, industriously doing up loose nuts. As one of them admitted, it was a hopeless effort, but one felt like doing *something*. (I borrowed a spanner and tightened a few myself.) Afterward, the Spanish officials presented each team with champagne as a token of thanks for this gesture.

When three drivers (Ickx, Roelof Wunderink and Bob Evans) appeared for the 2 p.m. Saturday practice, the clerk of the course personally thanked them. The remaining 23 held fast in their van.

At about a quarter to 4 p.m., when final practice was supposed to begin, the race organizers came to the van with a flat ultimatum of their own. The CSI observers said the circuit met FIA standards, therefore contracts must be honored, or there would be legal action; in that event the Spanish police, as a matter of course, would impound the equipment of the defaulting entrants pending litigation.

It was not necessary to look around the paddock: at the high walls of the stadium and its gates. Everyone understood the organizers had the entirety of Formula 1 racing at what could be literally gunpoint within seconds.

I kept a tally as in ones and twos the drivers emerged from their retreat and walked out to the pit lane. Soon enough every car but two was droning around the circuit. At 20 minutes past the hour Jochen Mass, his expression dark, climbed into his number. 2 Mclaren, and then there was only one man missing. The mechanics assigned to the World Champion's car were standing atop its tires, peering up the now crowded pit road.

At 4:35 the grandstand across the way erupted in whistles and boos and Emerson came into view, walking slowly, face set in stone. So that was all of them. The GPDA had broken.

It would have been enough, per the letter of the contract, to drive around slowly for three timed laps. That's what Fittipaldi did, rasping along in second gear with an arm in the air. Then he parked and walked away. It was perfectly clear he would not participate on Sunday.

If anyone else had begun that final practice session with the same idea, it was forgotten in the heat of the battle for grid positions, in the anxiety to get the car right for the race. They were racers, after all, born and trained and honed to race. But after it was over, Jody Scheckter stood looking down at his feet and said, "I suppose I was at about ten-tenths just now. This track is madness. Emerson is right. He's the only man among us."

The race? Yes, they went on and raced. It was a disaster. Nine cars piled up at the first corner. The survivors kept going, but not for long. Mechanical failures and collisions took out more cars, including a series of leaders. At lap 26 the leader happened to be Rolf Stommelen in one of Graham Hill's cars.

AUTOSPORT

Full report of the tragic Spanish Grand Prix

Bob Evans had his choice of Stanley BRMs, one fitted with the P200 type engine, both fitted with revised fuel injection.

Tom Pryce and Jean-Pierre Jarier were using their pair of accustomed UOP Shadows DN5s and there was a third brand new one available as a spare.

John Watson had his choice of two Matchbox Surtees, which were supplied with several different nose sections including a narrow one with Ferrari-type wing; this was not used.

The second driver to Merzario in the Williams team, given the absence of Laffite in the F2 world, was Tony Brise making his F1 debut in the ex-Merzario chassis. The young Formula Atlantic star had done some testing at Goodwood, and now in Spain the cockpit had been so modified that he was at least fairly comfortable.

At Embassy, the pair of Hills (with an old Lola as spare) were also graced with a new driver, Francois Migault replacing Graham himself alongside Rolf Stommelen. The Frenchman's face looked sadly battered about the mouth and nose — he'd fallen off a motorcycle.

...a trio of Heskeths this time, two in ... for James Hunt, both to ... Jones was

The dangerous barriers with bolts missing and the ...post. ...for the rather abrasive ...supply of

Jochen Mass was finally awarded victory in his Texaco Marlboro McLaren. He was the first to admit it was anything but a satisfactory or happy first ever GP w...

SPANISH GRAND PRIX/BARCELONA

Civil war in Spain

By PETE LYONS

Photos by DAVID WINTER
Race data by ALAN PHILLIPS

teams, there had been no opportunity of doing any testing. To cope with the Montjuich Park circuit, notoriously hard on brakes and transmissions, everyone of course fitted what they could in the way of large brakes with large-capacity air ducting, and took what steps they could to give the gearboxes an easy time. The generally slow cornering speeds meant large, steep aerofoils were called for.

Frank Williams had the one really new machine, his "FW 04" (sic) which, as was described in last week's A...

Pages from the author's contemporary race report in *Autosport.*

Standing in the pits, I heard a gasp and saw heads turn. Looking up the rise leading toward the first corner, I got an impression of dust, flying debris, slowing cars and something with a metallic sheen disappearing over the guardrail on the right just past the hillcrest. There was a heavy "crump" sound.

The leading Hill had suffered a structural failure of a carbon fiber strut supporting the rear wing. Spinning violently, the car hit the guardrail on the left side of the track, rebounded back, and went airborne as the road leveled off. It was a yard in the air as it reached the barrier, and only scraped the top rail as it went over. There was chainlink fencing beyond, but the car tore it down. Several people standing in and near a flag post there were hit, and four died. The driver suffered several broken bones.

It has to be noted that in this instance, as in every other crash that day, the guardrails performed as they were supposed to. Nothing pulled loose. It was only the lack of a higher barrier at the top of the hill that allowed the car to leave the circuit.

But blame could not be escaped. For several minutes I observed chaos, with the formally-attired officials at the startline standing about like penguins. I saw Niki Lauda, who had gone out in the first lap accident, run down and shout at them. But it took three laps for someone to shake out the checkered flag. Not before time, I felt.

Apparently the "winner," Jochen Mass, felt the same. He rolled in and erupted from his McLaren in a muscular fury, looking like he wanted to punch somebody, anybody, in a penguin suit.

People I trusted, who ran up to the accident scene and helped control the crowd and carry off injured, told me it was fully 10 minutes before any ambulance came.

That's how that race ended. It's the most stark example I can give of the state of disorganization that used to prevail in what we used to call the Grand Prix Circus. Is it any wonder that the businesslike, efficient, relentlessly ambitious Bernard Charles Ecclestone, who was there that day with his Brabham team, saw a power vacuum?

Pete pours for sisters (from left) Pat, Claire and Susan, ca. 1956.

Section 4

This and That

40

Between the Races

Vintage Racecar, October 2004

THE LAST CAR ends its cool-off lap, sending one last snap of delicious sound echoing away across the raceway. This is when another kind of fun begins.

In the quiet aftermath of a sports car race the other day, I was asking one of the younger pro drivers about how it had gone for him, but his mind was on his next adventure. The following event was close enough to get to by rental car, rather than taking one more airline flight, and Pacific Coast scenery he'd never seen would be worth the drive. Which route should he follow? What sights should he be sure to take in?

A pang of nostalgia overtook me. I used to be able to invest my time between races in quality travel, too.

In my footloose youth, which I suppose went on for a long time by conventional standards, I was a motorsports gypsy, and glad of it. There were enough races to cover to make a living, but not so many as to interfere with *living*.

When the race organizers had their acts together, my season's schedule was an orderly, logical progression between pins on the map. Some years I could start with Daytona, camp in my Econoline in the Keys until Sebring, drive back up to the East and Midwest for all the summer races there, and end the year with a great loop around the West.

Later on, covering F1, I'd follow the Circus to Argentina and Brazil for several weeks, go on across to South Africa, and then spend the entire summer enjoying Europe. In those days, North American GPs were properly placed on the calendar to bring me home at the end of the season.

A glance at the schedules shows they've got it all messed up nowadays. To cover racing as I used to, I'd have to live on commercial airplanes. And that's not my idea of living.

Do young journos today get to spend an off-weekend with a World Champion and his brother in their family vacation house on the coast of Brazil? I did once, with the Fittipaldis in Guaruja. There Emerson and Wilson took me for a stroll on the beach, which was thronged with girls in thongs. I was so amused at how much the brothers were getting out of the experience that I couldn't resist pointing out that one day Emerson's baby, Juliana, would be drawing just the same appreciative attention.

Emmo's mobile face darkened like a thunderstorm. "Eef those boys touch my Juliana, I *KEEL* them!"

Another day, in the Fittipaldi race shop across the street from the Interlagos track, Wilson got out his old Porsche 917 coupe and took me for a bloodcurdling ride at full scream around the residential neighborhood. I remember being crammed into a tiny capsule with my head bent over under the roof, trying to keep my arms and feet away from Wilson's, which were very busy. Every gear change snapped my neck. There was a savage noise chasing us from behind, and rosebushes and parked cars were whizzing by the high green fender domes. Madness, yes, but I believe I gained more appreciation of the 917's stupendous performance in that setting than had we been lapping the nearby track.

One year, Baron Huschke von Hanstein and the Baroness invited me to go along as they drove from Sao Paulo up the coast to Rio. *On the coast.* We actually drove on hard-packed beach sand for a long part of the way through spectacular tropical scenery. Nearing Rio, acting in his capacity as an FIA official, Huschke treated me to a tour of inspection of the new circuit there. It was not yet paved, so again we were driving on sand.

You gain so many insights when you have time to open your mind to them. If I'd had to fly back to some office after every race, I'd never have been able to stop off while driving through Switzerland one day to visit Jackie Stewart's home and watch his brain at work. I was traveling with a friend who had some business to conduct. It was conducted from lounge chairs by the swimming pool, but Jackie was not lounging.

While paying close and courteous attention to my friend and his proposal, the three-time World Champion was simultaneously proofreading and signing outgoing correspondence, dictating new letters and giving other instructions to his (bikini-clad) secretary Ruth, monitoring the telephone conversation his wife Helen (also bikini-clad) was having about that night's restaurant reservation, and also telling me stories and jokes, all at once, all without missing a beat, and without once making anyone feel they had less than his full attention.

I thought, that's the kind of brain it takes to win three F1 championships.

Had I not lived in a Microbus camper during the summer of '75, I would never have been sheltering from the rain in it with a friend one afternoon at Silverstone when Mark Donohue scurried by, did a double-take, and accepted our invitation to tea. He spent the better part of an hour with us, talking quietly about his unhappy F1 season but also ranging thoughtfully across many other topics.

I didn't tape record it. I didn't even take any notes. I didn't foresee how limited our time with him would be (he would die just weeks later). The clearest thing I retain from that conversation is my friend's assessment after he left. Her eyes wide, she exclaimed, "That man is *so intelligent!*"

This one chance encounter sums up how I'll always remember Mark.

I hope my young sports car racer from the other day fully enjoyed his drive up the coast. The sounds of racing are great. But so is the quiet between races.

41

Magic Tracks

Vintage Racecar, December 2004

SHANGHAI'S GAUDY NEW, $300 million supercircuit, home of the first-ever Grand Prix in China recently, has a truly distinctive first turn complex. It coils up tightly one way like a watch spring, then unwinds. It seems obvious to me it's meant to look like the oriental Yin Yang symbol.

SpeedTV commentators remarked that a diagram of the entire lap—which was drawn up by a European—deliberately resembles the Chinese character Shang, which they said means "to strive."

Well. Race track design as a graphic art.

I enjoyed that telecast. The circuit appeared to be racier than some new ones we've seen, and we've seen a lot of them recently; hooray to that. But while watching the race, I kept wondering: What is it that makes for a good race track, anyway?

By way of investigation, I started a list of the motorsports venues I've personally been to around the world. Places where I'd watched races, rallies, drags, hill climbs, trials, speed record attempts, ghymkhanas, rock crawling, any and every kind of motor vehicle competition. I included performance schools I've attended, and added pilgrimages I've made to sites where racing was held historically, but no longer. I did not include anyplace I've only seen on-screen.

The first 50 names came easily, and when I reached the 90s I got excited about trying to break 100. No problem. Thanks to my wife, who suggested several from her own experience that I'd forgotten, my tally currently stands at 174. We might think of more, but that's enough for analysis.

Going down the list, responding to nothing but gut feelings, I marked the standouts, those motorsports locales I remember with special fondness and would especially like to visit again—even if, in some sad cases, it could only be in memory.

Thirty-seven. That's my number of magic tracks.

What factors do they have in common? Fast turns? Ample passing zones? Nice landscaping? Well-equipped media centers with convenient parking? Good track food? Or did they stick in my mind for fabulous races I'd seen there?

Sometimes such points applied, sometimes none did, but in reviewing my choices, I realized they were not the primary factors that moved my pencil.

It's hills.

Thirty-five of the 37 venues that stand out in my heart have (or had) dramatically undulating terrain.

Well, I'm three-dimensional, and so are my favorite vehicles; tracks ought to be too. Flat ground is plain boring. But I'm serious. Rises and falls, dips and crests, what Piero Taruffi's classic book (on which I was raised) *The Technique of Motor Racing* called "vertical curves," add driving difficulty. Cars—and even more so bikes—handle differently as slopes change. Road racing appeals to me for its variety of challenges, and the third dimension multiplies that factor.

Varied terrain also adds to spectator enjoyment, creating more viewing angles and often more visual surprise. Photographers appreciate this aspect, too, and it certainly comes across on TV.

More important to me, though it's a bit more esoteric, is that hills expand my sense of scale. They make an artificial road course feel more like the "real thing," the great point-to-point highway races that are the foundation of my own enthusiasm. Road Atlanta and Laguna Seca are not the mountainous Mille Miglia or Carrera Panamericana, but when cars disappear over hillcrests on the little circuits I am able to

Niki Lauda, Ferrari, at the Nürburgring, 1974.

believe they're going somewhere. Much as I enjoy a good scrap on a short oval—and one dirt track did make my list of favorites—it's not the same feeling.

If you'd like to know what else is on my list, topping everywhere else is the old Nürburgring. I've gone on and on about that mythic dragon of a circuit many times before, and have no intention of stopping. The 'Ring is simply The One for me.

The Baja 1000 route also is on my list. So is the sadly defunct Bridgehampton, the later one with the hills. Donington. The Isle of Man. Mid-Ohio. Monaco. Mosport. Pikes Peak. St. Jovite. VIR.

I won't clutter this page with all 37 names, but I should mention one where the ground is as flat as an airfield, because it is one: Goodwood Motor Circuit. As I said, choices were made on gut feelings. I realize I just love the place, hills or no. Generous viewing embankments did help its case.

Shangahi? Bahrain? Magny Cours? I haven't been to these sterile-looking modern places. Nothing I see of them on TV inspires me to go.

But if time travel ever comes about, I'll sure flash back to the old Targa Florio.

42

Twins

Vintage Racecar, June 2005

EARLY IN THIS year's Sebring 12-Hour, the two technicolored Audis that would go on to dominate the day were romping around nose-to-tail, a pairing that made an irresistible target for my Canon. As I kept shooting them, lap after lap, I thought back on all the other "twins" that have burned their images into my memories.

Just seeing two identical cars isn't enough. There's lots of teams of those. To be immortal, twins have to stamp their times.

But what a lot of them have. Think of the Cunninghams and Scarabs in the 1950s, and then the Chaparrals in the early 1960s. Later that decade the Can-Am became the "Bruce and Denny Show" of twin McLarens. As that grand old series began to die in the '70s, it turned into the "George and Mark" Porsche Panzers, and later the "George and Ollie" Shadows. In the 1990s, the twilight of IMSA's GTP series was colored by what I called Gurney's Great Whites, two identical Toyota Eagles.

It happens throughout racing. There was a wonderful period in CART when my eyes loved watching Mario and Michael Andretti, twins right to their helmet colors. (And who can ever forget Mario's prideful, wistful TV spot about the first time Michael out-raced him: "Bye-bye, Da-da!") I remember Parnelli Jones and George Follmer going at each other in duplicate Trans-Am Mustangs, and

Jim Hall and Hap Sharp, Chaparral 2s, at Watkins Glen, 1964; that's the author just visible past the leading car's fender.

Pedro Rodriguez and Jo Siffert leaving tire marks on each other's Porsche 917s.

Today in F1 all the cars come two-by-two, though the two that stamp the modern era, at least up to this season, are the iridescent red Ferraris. But their drivers have to be equal to make cars true twins. Take away his teammate and Michael Schumacher would remain supreme, just as Juan Fangio or Jimmy Clark were in their eras, no matter who sat in cars painted like theirs.

Racing dominance does often come as a solo act. Mark Donohue's 1972 Indy victory and 1973 Can-Am championship are no less superb because he drove alone. And many racing eras are defined by titanic battles between machines that look nothing alike.

Yet there's something special about twins. I credit TV commentator Sam Posey for pointing this out late in an F1 event, as the camera lingered for a moment on a pair of team cars abandoned alongside one another. It was a strikingly painterly image and Sam, a talented painter, was moved to a mini-lecture on how the repetition of forms satisfies our souls.

Just so.

43

St. Jovite:
Lovely Le Circuit

Vintage Racecar, December 2005

RACING TRANSCENDS VENUE. I've done my time at grungy old bullrings, squalid street courses, insipid parking lots, sterile speedways, a forlorn airstrip whose primary enterprise seemed to be the drying of turkey manure; I've been to some really ugly race tracks and seen gorgeous racing regardless.

Yet how much more moving the experience can be when the facility itself has magic. High up on my own list of favorites is Canada's Le Circuit.

Call it that, or St. Jovite, or even Mount Tremblant; it answers to them all and to me it addresses everything I like about racing. First of all, it's in Quebec, meaning a trip there feels almost like going to Europe. You drive a mere 90 miles to the northwest of the Montreal metropolis into the Laurentian Mountain, pass the linked resort towns of St-Jovite and Mont-Tremblant, and find the 2.65-mile road course nestled amid woody hills under the highest peak in the region. The stream rushing by the first turn is *le Diable*—the Devil River.

On my first visit I found a marvelously plunging, twisting, tricky little lap with hardly any stretch of straight anywhere. The setting was pleasingly rustic, the flavor charmingly ramshackle. It struck me as a mini-Nürburgring, my most beloved circuit of all time. Le Circuit's first-turn complex, a seemingly never-ending right-hand bend that goes down and up and down, heavey-bumpy all the way, helped make this one of those tracks that vividly shows off the challenge of race driving.

Then there were the French-Canadian girls; wow. I loved this place on first sight, and always thought it must be a commercial success.

Alas, it wasn't. The track opened in 1964, and in 1966 it appropriately presented the very first round of the Canadian-American Challenge Cup series. What a cracker of a race that was, with John Surtees in a Lola just holding off the McLarens of Bruce McLaren and Chris Amon; two hours, six minutes of Big Banger sports car racing at its best.

That also was the race when St. Jovite became home field of the Can-Am Flying Club. During practice both Paul Hawkins and Hugh Dibley—an airline pilot—had their Lola T70s literally take off, their front-ends lifting over a certain hump and continuing to lift until the cars cartwheeled over backward, a stunt power boaters call

Denny Hulme, McLaren, starts from pole alongside Jackie Stewart, Lola, in the 1971 Can-Am.

a "blowover." Happily nobody was hurt, not then and not some years later when Jackie Oliver famously did the deed again in Peter Bryant's first Titanium Car. Subsequently the hump was cut down, just like the one at Le Mans has been.

The Can-Am skipped a couple of years, but was back in 1969 (winner Hulme, McLaren), 1970 (Dan Gurney, McLaren) and '71 (Jacky Stewart, Lola). Moments I remember from those races? How about Stewart's stirring battle with Hulme that last year, one of the few times we really saw hard Can-Am *racing*. Or the sight of undersung Canadian John Cordts fearlessly launching his McLaren over a sort of ski-jump; the sight made you want to run away. Then there was Lothar Motschenbacher's Ironman drive on the day he voluntarily started from the back of the grid because he was feeling ill (bad food was suspected) and didn't think he could last; not only did he last, he forged his way up to finish fifth, driving like a man in the pink of condition—but when it was all over he was visibly on the point of collapse.

In '68 and again in 1970, Le Circuit hosted the F1 Canadian Grand Prix. Denny Hulme won the first in a McLaren, Jacky Ickx the

Clay Regazzoni, Ferrari, in the 1970 Canadian Grand Prix.

second with Ferrari. Watching a GP at St. Jovite was a special treat, those vivid, snappish little cars slashing around like pirate cutlasses, scary and satisfying all at once. This was one of the few courses where F1s could lap faster than the big, all-powerful Can-Ams.

USAC's Indy cars came twice to put on four 100-mile races; Mario Andretti won them all. There was also an SCCA United States Road Racing Championship sports car race plus four Trans-Am sedan events, all five of them taken by Mark Donohue.

And then . . . the fire went out. After only 13 major events held in five years (according the track's present website), the big days were over. I remember hearing that the VIPs considered one of my favorite race tracks to be too rustic, too cramped, too far out of the way; they also called it too bumpy and, yes, dangerous. Hah. I presume it all came down to too little money fluttering around to suit their greedy commercial souls. Anyway, they robbed me of lovely little Le Circuit, which essentially lay fallow for long, dreary years.

It sounds like I'm building up to one more lament about Good Old Days Now Lost . . . but St. Jovite is still with us! Like VIR and Goodwood, it survived the dead years and now new money has come along to bring it back to life. Something that's right with our world.

From what I can tell without going there the track has been tastefully refurbished while preserving its character, widened (from 28 feet to 36—still darned narrow!) and altered in just a couple of places to improve safety. Among other events there's an important vintage meeting there now, and everybody raves about it (you can get detailed info plus a video ride at www.lecircuit.com). I long to go back.

44

Howl at the Moon

Vintage Racecar, March 2005

NIGHT RACING. Why do we love it so?

I think one reason is, darkness adds another dimension to the defiance. Motor racing has a deliciously illicit taste even in daylight, and doing it after sundown seems *sinful.*

Let us embrace that, I say. Sometimes when I mention to lay people that I like auto racing, they seem to recoil. It's as though I'd confessed a taste for trophy hunting, say, or warfare. But despite society's opinions, some of us admit racing satisfies us on a deep, primitive level. We see racers girding themselves in warrior armor and mounting powerful, willful battle steeds, all bedecked with colorful, totemic symbols, and sallying forth to glorious combat. Racing gets our blood up; it brightens our day.

Our night, too. Especially our night. Nighttime is when we diurnal beings know we ought to be holed up in caves, cowering. Our senses of sight, sound and smell are simply no match for those of hungry things that prowl the inky wilderness.

Or they weren't until we found fire, and figured out how to carry it around with us. Suddenly we owned the night. We were *free!*

It is that liberation we celebrate when driving behind headlights. Something at the bottom of our prehistoric minds is howling brave disdain at the dark.

But night racing also appeals on higher levels. Drivers report cars run stronger in the cool of the night, while crews and crowds appreciate the cool itself. And everybody appreciates the dramatic spectacle: the sweeping speed of the glaring lights, the seemingly more abrupt arrivals of the cars, the orange-hot brakes, the exhaust flames. It's a magical sound-and-light show, endlessly enchanting.

I think of night races as rare treats, but in fact we can see a lot of racing at night. The biggest, oldest sports car enduros feature hours of it. So does rallying, of course. More and more speedways have been installing floodlights for both stock car and open-wheel events, following the lead of promoters at the small ovals and drag strips who long ago realized their clientele likes to come after working hours.

Lighting up a whole road course would be tough, but sports and GT cars carry their own lights. Should open-wheelers do so too? A few years ago I saw just that proposal advanced to "save" the declining Champ Cars. That didn't happen, but maybe F1, which seems to be desperately trying everything else to boost itself, could

consider nighttime Grands Prix.* That should be very popular in hotter climes.

But what about being able to see sponsor signage, they'll protest. Well, F1 so enjoys throwing money at problems, just think of the advances in illumination technology that nighttime GPs might foster.

Illumination is indeed what night racing is all about. Drivers need it, of course, and so do photographers, but in a different way. Back in the 1950s, when my dad started taking me to Sebring, we basically shot until the sun got low, then put away the cameras. Film emulsions of the day just weren't sensitive enough to make sharp images in twilight, and after dark the only things you'd see on the film would be scattered headlight-specks. Exhaust flames were too dim and fleeting to catch—I tried a few times with no decent result—and drum brakes didn't glow.

Yes, dad sometimes did pit lane work with a flash gun, but I didn't have one of those, so for me night racing was a blend of enjoyment of the sights and frustration that I couldn't capture them.

In later seasons, as I found faster film and as both cars and trackside environs seemed to provide more light, I began experimenting more and coming home with more pictures that pleased me (among many, many that didn't). But having to wait until the film was processed continued to be a downer. By the time I saw a successful picture, I'd forgotten how I achieved it.

Then . . . digital cameras appeared. Oh, frabjous joy! Immediate review of one image lets me improve the next, right on the spot, and suddenly even I can feel like a photographic success story!

And this has happened just as sports car endurance racing is in a boom time, with lots of night racing for lots of beautifully evil-looking cars with gaudy reflective graphics and lovely bright brakes.

So let that ol' sun go down. I'm howlin', man.

Written before Singapore inaugurated F1 night racing. I'm still waiting for my honorarium.

45

Confronting Demons

Vintage Racecar, February 2007

I DIDN'T SEE the accident happen, and it was many laps later when my photo trek around South Africa's Kyalami circuit brought me to the blackened wreckage. Thanks to the public address speakers I knew Clay Regazzoni was alive. Still, his burned-out BRM was a grisly sight and I thought it should be documented. I lifted my camera.

Something sharp struck just below my right shoulder blade. Out of the crowd behind had sailed a flattened drink can.

In a rage, I picked it up and whirled around, looking for someone to retaliate against. But several thoughts tangled in my brain at once, staying my hand.

One, I didn't spot a likely culprit; everyone seemed to be avoiding my eyes. Two, hurling the missile back would surely escalate the confrontation—the farm-style wire fence would have been no barrier to angry young toughs.

And three, under my heat I felt empathy. These innocent spectators, out for a good day's motor racing, had witnessed a hideous thing. In their eyes, perhaps, I was a soulless *paparazzo* bent on profiting from near-tragedy. We were all on edge, I realized. The ugly underside of racing in those days was drawing much criticism, jeopardizing the sport we all loved.

So I contented myself by turning my back and ostentatiously taking my time over several carefully framed photos of the car. Nothing more was thrown. My own emotion cooled. In my race report, I sank only to the level of referring to the crowd as "a rude lot."

And I never submitted the photos for publication, not before now.

That incident happened in 1973, my first full year following the whole F1 series, and I was a bit wide-eyed and breathless about it all: tramping the wondrous raceways of the world, mingling with the GP greats, watching their magical driving week after week, getting to intimately know their fabulously high-strung, savage little weapons . . . .

The Regazzoni crash was disturbing, but he'd gotten out all right, assisted by fellow driver Mike Hailwood, who'd been involved but earned hero status by running into the fire to help. No real harm done, and I had a colorful story with a happy outcome.

Ten races into that year, during the Dutch GP at Zandvoort, a newcomer named Roger Williamson hit a guardrail, which leaned back in the soft, sandy soil and formed a spiraling launching ramp, flipping his March over. Again flames erupted, and again a fellow driver waded into them. But brave David Purley was unable to right the car on his own and, according to several witnesses, the marshals on the scene did not attempt to assist. Williamson burned to death.

Then in practice for the year's final GP, the U.S. at Watkins Glen, Francois Cevert was killed when his Tyrrell slammed into the same kind of barrier. Here, the steel rails separated and knifed the aluminum monocoque apart like tinfoil.

Thankfully, I did not witness these crashes either. But my imagination effortlessly painted the pictures, adding two more horrors to the many already crammed into my uneasy conscience. Uneasy, because this activity that I was in effect promoting with every written word had already destroyed people I had counted as personal friends: Walt Hansgen, Bruce McLaren, Pedro Rodriguez, Jo Siffert, Swede Savage, others.

Yet in those days deadly risk was widely held to be an integral part of the game. "Motor racing is dangerous, it's made like that," Jacky Ickx once calmly remarked to me. In the opinion of many "aficionados," the danger somehow elevated the sport to the rarified level of romantic, Hemingwayesque esteem long attached to mountaineering, bullfighting, and war.

A really good driver will avoid accidents, was the complacent attitude.

Resistance to change is inbred in human beings, and reluctance to adopt safety measures is as old as racing itself. Even what now-scanty-looking equipment was in common use by 1973, relatively primitive helmets, fireproof clothing, seat belts, roll bars, all had been fought at some stage.

One component of the resistance was aesthetic: when first proposed, such things as roll bars looked clumsy, spoiling the beauty of existing, highly-developed cars. Think of the general public's opinion of the first "safety bumpers" on passenger vehicles. In either case, few people at the time could visualize how elegantly integrated such structures would ultimately become.

There was also self-interest. I believe Phil Hill has explained the line of thinking in his era was that no professional racer wanted to acknowledge the danger because it would give aid and comfort to anti-racers, who might then ban his livelihood.

And there was simple denial—don't speak the name of the demon lest it appear.

Of course that didn't keep it from appearing.

Another Jackie, world champion Stewart, who had been Cevert's teammate and close friend, and who had lost other friends to racing, had different feelings entirely. Tirelessly, against often bitter opposition, he was trying to change thinking about safety.

I used to get into arguments about all this, but not because my mind was settled. I was drawn both ways. On the one hand, I remember emoting to fellow journo Peter Windsor that the inherent danger made a driver's performance more important than in other sports, thus making racing more meaningful. As Michael Andretti put it to me a few years later, "In ball games, if you drop the ball, you drop the ball. If we drop the ball, we hit the wall."

Peter didn't buy that at all, maintaining stoutly that he would be perfectly satisfied to admire brilliant driving free of the slightest risk.

But after I wrote something about the need to "police ourselves, or we will be policed," pointing out that climbers "do not go onto the mountain with bad rope," my boyhood hero Denis Jenkinson confronted me angrily. "If we carry what you say to the end, we'll give *up* motor racing!"

Conflicted myself, I understood his anxiety. We both were loathe to lose any of the elements of racing that had excited us in the first place. Yet I am sure Jenks had no more desire to keep on writing obituaries than I did.

We had to, though. Early in 1974 we wrote about Peter Revson, my Can-Am friend Revvie, killed in testing at Kyalami. That fall Helmuth Koenigg died at Watkins Glen.

The following season seemed to be going fine until Austria, when Mark Donohue was fatally injured. That really hurt me.

It hurt despite the fact that, in those days, in my case, one tried not to get too close. Approximately 30 participating drivers per F1 season, one or two fatalities each year . . . bad odds. I vividly remember having a pitlane conversation with someone, who then climbed into his car and drove away, and through the engine's scream I distinctly heard the words in my mind, "I wonder if I'll ever talk with him again."

That stress was one of several reasons I eventually quit F1 reporting.

Times have changed. Jackie Stewart's views prevailed—even with me. Step by step (though some proved to be missteps) racing has been made safer. Today, fatalities are so infrequent they shock us. No, we didn't have to "give up motor racing." There's more of it today than ever and, though you'll often hear us geezers gripe about one sorry thing or another, I cannot honestly claim that modern racing at its best is any less interesting and exciting than in "my day."

Bottom line, I wish Mark and Revvie and all the rest were still here to enjoy it.

46

Bikes

Vintage Racecar, April 2007

AH, SPRING, WHEN a lad's fancy turns to thoughts of . . . well, what do you suppose? Taut curves. Deep breathing. Throbbing . . . .

Yes, we're talking motorcycles, of course. I'm not sure what's happening to me, but recently my brain has been brimming with bikes.

Quite against my will. Although I was long a keen motorcyclist, and have many fond memories of marvelous rides all over North America and Europe, I gave up riding in a conscious, determined effort to mature. Bikes just don't fit my life now. I don't have time for one, let alone a place—the family snowblower takes up the only possible spot.

Even if I got another motorcycle, perhaps justifying it by fuel savings as many people are today, in reviewing trips I regularly make I can't identify one that actually would make sense on two wheels.

What about casual sport riding? Truly, I don't have time. Nor do I find modern highway conditions much fun.

The last bike I had, I had for four years and rode precisely twice. I liberated it to someone more worthy of it. Obviously, I don't *deserve* a motorcycle.

Yada yada. Spring is coming and I can't stop thinking about motorcycles.

My interest in them goes back to 1953, when my dad took me to the big annual road race at Laconia, New Hampshire. A few years later, just as I was learning to drive cars, Ozzie came home one day with a classic British V-twin called a Vincent and proceeded to teach me about bikes as well. My education on it included a complete cross-country ride, New York to California. I went on to buy eight motorcycles of my own. So far.

Last month, going on about British vehicles, I mentioned a Triton I briefly owned, and I'd like to show you what mine ought to have been. Pictured here is a Triumph-Norton special that riveted me in my boots one summer's day in 1969, at the Bridgehampton Can-Am.

Isn't it sweet? The Triumph Bonneville engine nestles so neatly in the Norton Featherbed frame, combining the one's (relatively) reliable, smooth power with the other's renowned (for its day) roadholding and precise steering. See that lovely aluminum tank, sculpted for tucking-in? Those graceful pipes, swept back for cornering clearance? That muscular, two-leading-shoe front brake, and the light, strong alloy rims? I love how this single-seater is so spare, so efficient, so pure-of-purpose—it's leaning against the truck because, to save weight, there's no prop-stand.

That perfect motorcycle haunted my dreams for approximately half a year. Then I saw my first four-cylinder Honda. At Daytona in 1970, I watched Dick Mann win the 200 aboard a stripped-down, hopped-up CR750 with the most magnificent quartet of gracefully sweeping exhaust pipes. Those pipes haunted my dreams for another half a year, until that fall, when I succumbed to a sparkling red-and-gold production model CB750 of my very own.

I rode straight from the dealership to a burger stand, taking care to park where I could gaze at those glorious pipes as I munched. I remember that as one of the most fulfilling moments of my life.

To me, motorcycles have more personality than cars. I realized this on the black morning I found my Triumph 650 stolen. The affront was so personal, I wanted to KILL. I've not yet owned a car that would have brought up the same rage.

That bike was recovered (no, nobody died), but later was taken again, this time permanently. Must have been a great bike.

Motorcycles have more personality, I think, because they're smaller, lighter, meant primarily for solo use, and they're naked. Even when wrapped up in fairings, you feel very exposed on a bike, very much dependent on your own skills and wits. Your single-track steed is more your partner than any four-wheeler. Certainly there is risk, and that's part of why riding a bike on the road gives me a sense of adventure that it takes a race track to make me feel in cars.

And it takes a very high-end car to match the technical appeal of everyday motorcycles. I was always proud that my Honda four, a world-changing breakthrough in its time, had an overhead cam and hemi heads, "just like" classic Ferraris. Today's road bikes bristle with technology developed in racing, all those exotic things we all love about the most exciting automobiles, yet it's all affordable to an everyday motorcycle enthusiast.

You can see it all, too. Open the hoods of many cars today; can you actually spot an engine under all the plastic?

So far I haven't even mentioned performance, but . . . *sheesh!* Feel smug about your really fast street car? If you haven't clamped your knees around a hyperbike and yanked it open, you have *NO IDEA* what real acceleration is.

The prime appeal to me about bikes, though, is their elegance. They're simply neat and tidy in an engineering sense. Like a formula race car, but more so, there's no more to motorcycles than there needs to be. Watching them single-track along their economical way is deeply satisfying to me.

In racing, bikes seem more honest than today's cars. Four-wheel competitors are constantly complaining about the difficulty of overtaking, but to riders the same tracks are generously wide and aerodynamic turbulence is much less troublesome.

Where could this line of thinking take me? One place is www.ahrma.org, the Web site of the American Historic Racing Motorcycle Association. There's some fun going on there.

I don't suppose Dick Mann's Daytona winner is available, but there must be a vintage class for a nice Triton.

47

Stacks 'n' Pipes

Vintage Racecar, May 2007

PERFORMANCE PERV THAT I AM, naked race cars turn me on. Even partially undressed ones. Lift an engine cover, unveil a shapely suspension arm, merely de-Dzus an access panel and I'm there, slavering. I simply groove on racing's luscious secret places.

That's probably one more reason I so fondly remember the Swinging Sixties, when quite often you could see a race car prance boldly into the public gaze with its intake stacks and/or exhaust headers, maybe even its whole engine, all beautifully bare and unashamed.

Modern designers hide all the good stuff under acres of modesty panels. It's for aerodynamics, they say, but, Hah. These people are just loveless prudes.

Can-Am intakes; those were the best stacks. Massive engines called for mighty injectors and they typically towered over the car itself, giant constructs of flared horns and intricate castings and complex linkages. They so dominated the car that when you were aboard—I've had that delight—it was their heavy rattling sound you heard, not the exhaust roar.

From the pits, engine tuners could visually monitor their charge's health by watching for "standoff" atop the stacks. This was a nimbus of raw fuel carried back out by air bouncing off the closed intake valve. Excessive standoff signaled a broken valve rocker. Rockers broke a lot in the Can-Am days.

Big-block Chevies, the Can-Am' s signature engines, generally wore "staggered" stacks, where four intakes were taller than the their neighbors. That's because the semi-hemi cylinder head had different intake passage patterns for adjacent cylinders, so resonance effects in stacks of equal external length resulted in two big humps in the torque curve. Staggering the stacks filled in the valley between the humps, giving the driver much smoother acceleration off the turns.

Those intakes really did look mutant, though, "like outrageous irradiated flowers," I remember writing. Part of the appeal of what, in those days, were the fastest road racers on earth.

For the best exhaust pipe fix you had to go an open-wheeler race. In the days of front engines, GP and Indy cars usually had long side-pipes so distinctive they were part of the model's identity. Think of the Offy Roadsters, Maserati's 250F, the 1956 Lancia-Ferrari D50—artwork showing nothing other than those exhaust systems probably would bring the car's name to your mind instantly.

With the move to rear engines it got even better. Auto Union's V-16 and later V-12 engines emitted their staccato bellows through bristling arrays of individual, vertically-curled stub exhausts like so many Viking helmet horns. BRM applied the same simple system to its first 1.5-liter V-8, and so did Jim Hall and Hap Sharp on their first mid-engined Chaparrals. Top Fuel dragsters maintain the splendid tradition to this day.

Pipes can merge for harmonic reasons and also gain on aesthetics. That little F1 jewel of the early '60s, the 1.5-liter Coventry-Climax V-8, wore an eight-into-two "crossover" system that terminated in long megaphones like tail guns on a B-17. Ford adopted the same idea on its DOHC Indy engine, but enhanced the visual statement with an intricately writhing "bundle of snakes" header system. These burst out of the top of the engine, from between the cylinder V, while the intakes jutted out from between the camshafts. Salacious stacks *and* pipes in one giddy voyeur's glance.

So much a part of the presentation was this Indy car exhaust plumbing that teams finished them in various colors of high-temperature

paint; I remember reds and blues and golds particularly.

Ferrari restrained itself to using just white paint with its F1 "top-pipe" V-12, but that was still a magnificent-looking beast. Its 12-into-4 exhaust system alone ought to be on my office wall.

As for one of the all-time most beautiful F1 cars, Gurney's Eagle, its gloriously naked Weslake was another to proudly show off both its 12 petite intake horns and its long, long quad-tailpipe system. The fire inside used to turn the titanium material the loveliest colors.

Ah . . . the wild old days when cars were young and innocent.

Summer of '57

Vintage Racecar, July 2007

BET YOU'RE THINKING of Fangio's transcendent victory at the 'Ring. The launch of the Fuelie Corvette. The beautiful Scarabs. Jaguar's fifth win at Le Mans, the third in a row for the immortal D-type. That year saw the end of the Mille Miglia, but Sputnik went up then too.

For sure, 1957 was a year of milestones, but what made it really special for me was getting my driver's license and then helping my dad drive his 1936 Rolls-Royce Phantom II clear across the United States, from New York to the West Coast. And then all the way back. "Crash-box" transmission and all.

Ozzie, trained as an engineer, admired any car of quality but was particularly drawn to the Rolls. During his youth in the 1920s and '30s these superbly crafted machines orbited the uppermost stratosphere of society, but by the 1950s few people saw value in them. They were thought too massive, too difficult to handle, too archaic. When Pop found the car of his dreams early in 1957, what once had been the imposing, chauffer-driven town conveyance of a Boston Brahman was a quaint, 21-year-old relic. It became ours for no more than the price of a decent used Chevy.

The classic car world then was very different in every way, compared to now. Owners like my dad worked on their own cars, aided and abetted by fellow enthusiasts. Ozzie and his good friend

Fred Kelly, who also had a PII, spent many happy, grimy hours under each other's cars, sometimes towing each other's cars, and prowling junkyards, hunting parts.

Sam Adelman had the best classic junkyard in our area. He was a wonderful old Russian who seemed to regard Rolls-Royces as royalty and his duty as upholding the respect due them in their dotage. Once he caught me on my knees peering under a running board, studying the chassis. "Mine boy, mine boy!" Sam scolded me. "A chentlemun does not look under a lady's skirt!"

In those days Rolls owners like Ozzie and Kelly, and many of their friends who had other makes, used their classics almost like everyday cars. Dad really did drive his Phantom II to work just about every day for years, and also joined his fellows for many a weekend "meet" or "tour." So it didn't really seem too extraordinary a notion—to us—to load up the family that first summer and jaunt off to California.

To prepare we special-ordered a set of brand-new Dunlops from England. I forget the size but in memory they seem about as tall as I

Ozzie and Pete lashing valves on the Rolls; note reflection of Gerry (mom) taking the picture.

was. That gave Ozzie confidence to remove one of the two spare wire wheels from a front fender and employ its sturdy anchor to hold an ice chest and water cooler.

The six of us insisted on bringing too much luggage for the trunk, which was an actual, separate, seaman's-style trunk hung from the back of the car. So dad engineered and built a roof platform. To mount it he asked a friend with a lathe to make four struts to replace the upper door-hinge pins. The idea proved trouble-free throughout our trip.

I think we took a whole month and covered 7,000 miles. Not fast miles; if you insisted on speed the grand old lady would lift her skirts and scamper to 70 or more, but about 50 was her comfortable cruising gait.

You felt like a king at the wheel. It was a big, black plastic wheel thrumming mildly in your hands as it reported every nuance of the road's texture passing far below. The system's only power was yours, of course, and our laden weight must have topped four tons, but the steering was uncannily light and responsive. The great vehicle felt poised, balanced, a thoroughbred. Gazing out along that long, long "bonnet" I enjoyed daydreaming I was racing a Bentley at Le Mans.

About that gearbox: the shift lever was a finely machined delight, long in length but very short in movement, and you could feel the oily mechanism down there through the skin of your fingers. You could also feel there was nothing but gears, *sans* synchromesh. To make a silent change—it could be done, it was *supposed* to be done—took perfect coordination and timing with gas, clutch and stick, double-declutching both up and down. Every time you achieved a quiet "snick" you felt proud. My father mastered it, but my success ratio was about one in 20. We both thought it best I not drive in the mountains.

It was the first time any of us had been beyond Ohio, and what a splendid escapade it was: the Rockies, Yosemite, Disneyland . . . .. I suppose our side-locker and roof bundle made us look like Okies, but natives were friendly. "You're a long way from home!" everybody who noted our New York plates wanted to inform us. None could properly pronounce "Rolls-Royce," but all knew it had a "sealed engine." Untrue, but what can you do about common knowledge.

Looking back at that milestone summer, I wonder how big a role this hands-on adventure with dad's fabulous old Phantom played in stoking and shaping my just-ignited passion for motorsports. I hadn't liked cars until I was taught to drive them, but now I *loved* cars. Although Ozzie's Rolls was in no way a performance car, your own performance in driving it mattered. Precision, sensitivity, awareness were vital. I think that experience established my whole approach to driving ever afterward.

Fifty years, now. That's how long I've had this delicious disease.

48

A Trophy from Riverside

Vintage Racecar, September 1999

PSSST ... CAN WE share a confidence? I just stole a piece of Riverside International Raceway. It's next to my keyboard right now, a chunk of old, brittle asphalt roughly 5 inches across, and exactly 3 3/8 inches thick. On the flat top of it, the former track surface, the small, irregular stones appear polished.

I like to think I helped polish them.

Many can say the same. RIR was an important place for a long time. Opened in 1957, this purpose-built road course surfed the contemporary wave of enthusiasm for sports car racing. Its location was pretty good, too, convenient to one of the world's biggest, most energetic communities, and to Hollywood.

Riverside staged the first big-time professional road race in the West (the 1958 Times Grand Prix), put on the second-ever Formula 1 GP of the U.S. (1960), and regularly brought NASCAR and USAC stars to their California fans. SCCA's "unlimited" Can-Am cars thundered there. So did IMSA's high-tech GTPs. Riverside also was a home to motorcycle, kart, and dragster racers. Between major promotions the track hosted countless club events, driver's schools, manufacturer and media tests and demos, and movie and TV productions.

My personal Riverside history began with that 1960 USGP. I clearly recall watching Stirling Moss sling a spidery little dark-blue

Lotus through the Esses to victory. Seven years later, I witnessed a wonderful Can-Am battle between Bruce McLaren and Jim Hall. I was there for every subsequent round of the grand old series, plus many other kinds of race.

It was at Riverside in 1971 that Can-Am champ Peter Revson gave me one of the rides of my life in his McLaren M8F. Other years brought other hot laps alongside the likes of Chris Amon, John Morton, Jim Busby, and Eddie Lawson. I even track-tested a March GTP at Riverside—more a test of me than the car—and twice did some racing on the school level in Formula Fords.

And I watched Riverside die. I saw a giant dam of dirt blockade the mighty Esses. I saw a heap of steel scrap glittering in the sun where garages once sheltered the greatest racing machines on this planet. A friend moved into a new townhouse smack atop what had been the "mile-long straight," where Revvie had taken me to 190 mph. I did not go visit.

Riverside was declared dead in 1988, and for the past 11 years I've thought the body was totally buried. Oh, I heard rumors of remnants, but several times I've driven past or flown over the site, looking for something identifiable. Nothing.

I wasn't looking hard enough. Keep this between us, but there really are bones to be found out there. The experience is eerie.

It was typically hot and hazy the July afternoon my wife and I approached the old place, so memories flowed easily. We described them to each other, and agreed we were visualizing the same Riverside Raceway. So we both felt the same shock as we turned down the familiar freeway exit at Day Street, and discovered that what had been a narrow, raggedy access road is now a multi-lane, landscaped parkway. Glossy corporate offices seem to have landed like alien spacecraft in what we remember as empty fields. Where we "saw" grandstands rising in memory, our actual eyes beheld the tacky sprawl of a mall.

As if by mental braille, we felt our way to what had been the shabby competitors' entrance. "Look," exclaimed Lorna, "That's where registration used to be." It's a prettified mobile home sales lot now.

Start of the 1972 Can-Am at Riverside; banked Turn 9 in background.

"OK," replied I, "so the press tower must have been . . .?" My voice trailed off uncertainly. You drove downhill to get there, but we were going up. They've changed the very shape of the ground.

This was more than disorienting. We felt displaced in time-space. Alternate-universe stuff. The eyescape of stucco condos, trimmed shrubbery and artistically arced service streets seemed to be a mirage overlaying the true desert terrain beneath.

But while most of the old RIR really is obliterated, the extreme south end is still "unimproved." Don't say I told you to ignore the "No Trespassing" signs, but, heck, the gates are standing open and kids are riding bikes all across this weedy wasteland.

The kids probably don't know they're wheeling over the ghost of one of international motor racing's famous corners, the wide, banked, scary-fast Turn 9.

We Outbacked over dirt ruts to a hillock, and got out. It was quiet. The heated air pressed on us. Sun-seared brush and grass seemed to be cowering under the glare of the ashen sky. That's right, I thought to myself, Riverside never was a garden spot. It was a raw place for a raw business.

For a moment, it was impossible to get our bearings. Then Lorna pointed out a distant line of cement shimmering in the heat. Was it part of the track wall opposite the old pits?

Below us, in a gully littered with other discarded items, we spotted mounds of dark material. We walked down. Asphalt. Broken and wrinkled and cracked like congealed lava, this rubble must have been the actual skin of Riverside International Raceway.

Beyond, we found several steel posts jutting from the ground. Still attached were fragments of steel plate, their edges bubbled and blackened by a cutting torch. A few remaining flecks of white and red paint, as well as the curving orientation, proved we'd found the infamous boiler plate wall around the outside of the turn. I remember whizzing by just beneath it, apprehensive.

There was a short stretch of ancient asphalt here too, cracked into chunks half-covered in sandy dust, but still in its old place on the smooth cant of the banking. I plucked a piece out, and held it up in the sun. The little polished stones winked at me. "Dan polished these," I thought, "and Mario and Jackie. Denny. Mark. Jimmy. Revvie . . . and I."

I don't know why these things mean so much to me. Nor do I understand why, to so many people, they appear to mean nothing. But I will forever cherish this small black nugget.

Don't bother trying this today, a dozen years later. Obliteration has continued and now there really is nothing left of the old track. But, no, my Asphalt Trophy is not for sale!

When power was unlimited: a Can-Am Chevy in a McLaren at Watkins Glen, 1972.

Section 5

Rants

Prototypes . . . of What?

Vintage Racecar, September 2001

A SUDDEN SNARL under my elbow, the mighty baritone of a big, twin-cam six with open pipes. Then a flash of pale green: four bold, beautifully teardrop-shaped fenders.

It's an Aston!

No—*THE* Aston! The very Aston Martin DBR1 that won Le Mans in 1959! Knifing through everyday traffic here in the city of Le Mans in 2001!

For just a moment we were side by side. I looked down from my utilitarian passenger vehicle into the open cockpit of a living, breathing Le Mans racer from yesteryear. I glimpsed a nest of stout steel frame tubes and a delicate wood-rim steering wheel quivering, alive, in the driver's fingers. I noticed the wind ruffling his hair . . . and that of his passenger.

His passenger. There was a second lucky devil in there, going along for (I supposed) the ride of his life.

Their brusque exhaust note as much as their startling, unsheathed-weapon appearance cleared their way, and they darted ahead, whisked around a street corner and were gone. But for a long, delicious moment I could still hear that magnificent engine sound reverberating back through the city canyon.

As perhaps you can tell, it's still reverberating in my mind. That was only one incident of a race weekend jammed full of memorable incidents, and others soon shouldered it aside. But now, as I peer into the pearly mystery of my computer screen, it is the Aston I see.

And its passenger. The DBR1's passenger is what has me thinking about today's Le Mans Prototypes.

I had come to France for the modern event, of course, but I could not deny myself a side trip into the past. A 45-minute "Le Mans Legend" supporting event scheduled for Saturday morning had drawn more than 60 vintage racers, many of them actual veterans of the 24-hour classic.

As part of the show these old-timers were being scrutineered in the old way, in the middle of the medieval Old City in a square below a pretty fountain.

Most of them got there in the old way, too, driven on the open highway. Lucky timing let me briefly share the street with that Aston, but at another moment it could have been the Talbot-Lago that won the 1950 race, or a Ferrari, a Maserati, a Lister, or any of a horde of Jaguars present that glorious weekend.

Mostly C-types plus a few Ds, the Jaguars had come to commemorate the 50th anniversary of the marque's first victory at La Sarthe, in 1951. They'd arrived *en masse* here in Le Mans' *Place du Jet d'Eau* after a brisk 40-mile run up from Tours.

"It was magnificent!" one American participant exclaimed. A collector from San Antonio, Julio C. Palmaz went on to tell me he also has an Ecurie Ecosse D-type, but elected to bring his C as more suitable. Originally raced by Giuseppe Farina, the first World Champion, this car was later driven by Dr. M.R.J. Wyllie to victory in the Seneca Cup at Watkins Glen.

Julio and 16-year-old son Chris, himself a kart and Formula Ford racer, were having a ball cruising their vintage British firebreather through the sun-drenched French countryside.

So was Sir Stirling Moss. While obligingly giving autographs to dozens of milling people, he told me about the C-type he was driving, the actual 1953 Le Mans winner. He also confirmed the old stories about the "works" Jaguars being driven out from Coventry on the public roads, to race and usually to win at Le Mans. My map indicates that would have been something like 350 highway miles. Two-lane highways, mostly, before motorways and autoroutes, town-to-town—*through* the towns.

"When I think back, it's amazing," Moss remarked. "To think of taking a racing car and driving it all the way from Coventry to here.

But that's what Jags did. They just put trade plates on."

That was indeed a different era, just as Le Mans was a different kind of race. "The French were very difficult on regulations, particularly with us," Stirling continued, "and they were always seeing whether you had a large-enough luggage space. B'cause this was supposed to be a race for Grand Touring cars, really . . . .'"

I was spellbound. This hero of my youth was talking about racing as it was when my youthful passion for it first ignited. My professional assignment lay at the track, where waited garagefuls of modern cars called Le Mans Prototypes and Grand Touring Prototypes. But this refreshing re-acquaintance with vintage models made me wonder anew:

What are today's "P-cars" supposed to be "Prototypes" of?

Sure, the Audis, Bentleys, Courages, and others are fabulous racing machines, exquisite works of engineering art capable of incredible performance.

The Audi R8 in particular—presently the dominant design—is a marvel to watch in action: powerful, smooth, well-mannered, reliable, remarkably rugged and very, very fast. It's so far ahead of its current competition that I call it the Silver Spaceship.

But where does it take us? Is this a prototype of some future Audi sports roadster, one which will put a mid-mounted turbocharged V-8, carbon-fiber chassis and other advanced technologies into the eager hands of the everyday (if well-heeled) enthusiast? Not likely.

As for the race car itself, 50 years from now, or even five, are you going to see a father and son jauntily touring Europe in a vintage Audi R8? Sorry, boy, you won't fit. There's simply not enough room in the "passenger" side for even a small one.

And your luggage? Le Mans dropped that requirement decades ago.

No, it saddens me to inform you that today's P-car is a prototype of nothing but next year's incrementally improved P-car. Which is all well and good for the racing, I suppose, if racing is no more than a clinical technical exercise devoid of romance, of dreams. That seems to be the trend; evidently sterility suits today's racing industry.

But what about the rest of us? We dreamers are drawn to racing because, secretly or not, we long to drive those marvelous race cars, or at least to have a fast ride in one.

And not necessarily on the race track. Haven't you ever daydreamed of the perfect high-speed "Grand Tour" over the gnarliest of open roads in the most fabulous of cars? Wouldn't you say, therefore, that "prototype" sports or GT race cars ought to be designed so they could, in fact, roar out of the race track and blast away across the landscape? Carrying two people? And maybe just a bit of their baggage?

We used to have such Le Mans cars, back in the C-type's day, but not so long ago we briefly had them again: the GT1s. I have driven a GT1 car, a McLaren, and I have enjoyed a fast track ride in another, a Mercedes. The good fortune has also been mine to drive a vintage C-type Jaguar—yes, on the public highway. Indelibly delectable experiences all, I assure you. These are what supersports enthusiast cars should be. They're the kind of car that drive their way into your daydreams, that live on to become vintage icons.

And cars that one day, with luck, will thrill a race fan who refuses to let go of the dream.

Where are the Brutes?

Vintage Racecar, April 2004

RECENT DISCUSSION in these pages about a supposed sixth Grand Sport racing Corvette rang two bells with me. First, I can confirm at least part of the story. Zora Duntov himself once told me that he'd built an extra GS, in secret, for Chevrolet engineers to play with.

But he ordered—no other verb for it—that I not talk about it. He meant to hold the revelation for a book he was planning. As I was involved in the plan at the time, I acquiesced.

I guess my orders expired with the man, and anyway, the book is out now. The project was finished by Zora's friend Jerry Burton, who does mention six prototype Grand Sports (page 284, *Zora Arkus-Duntov: The Legend Behind Corvette*, Bentley Publishers 2002). A few pages later, though, Burton repeats conventional wisdom by saying only five were completed. At the time he was writing, he could no longer consult Duntov. (Nonetheless, Jerry's is a painstaking look at a gifted but ornery man even more interesting than his cars; a good read available at www.BentleyPublishers.com.)

That second bell I hear is a question: whatever happened to big, brutal, terrifying race cars like Grand Sport Corvettes?

I still can see Zora's old racer's eyes sparkling as he described test-driving the first GS. It packed so much power in such a light frame, it literally hoisted its own front end off the ground. "Veelstendink!" he exclaimed; that was "wheelstanding" in his heavy Russian accent.

We used to have lots of wonderfully overpowered race cars like that. Think of the Cobras, Duntov's target with his Grand Sports. Think of the bellowing Scarabs and other American-engined specials, or the vastly powerful (for their times) 4.5 Maseratis and 4.9 Ferraris. But even they paled against the legendary supercharged, dope-drinking Auto Union and Mercedes Grand Prix monsters of the 1930s, which were rated as high as 646 horsepower.

That famous figure long stood as the high mark in road racing, but then the Can-Am came along with its unlimited engines, and soon 735 horsepower McLaren-Chevys were almost commonplace. We felt overwhelmed again when the turbocharged Porsche "Panzer" topped 950, then 1100. Later, briefly, USAC and F1 turbo cars were allowed to make that much and maybe more.

Those of us who had the great fortune to witness any of those ultra-powerful machines in action will never forget how they made the air tremble. Trying to follow their acceleration would almost snatch your eyeballs out.

Make us step back in fear when it fires up; that's what a real race engine is supposed to do, I say.

Please don't mistake me. I love all competition vehicles, and even the smallest, lowest-powered ones have undeniable charm. Bugattis were such elegant beauties. The early Lotuses were so gracefully delicate. Porsches started out as heroic giant-killers. Power and speed aren't as meaningful as function and efficiency. I've stood enraptured by a tiny, 50cc racing motorcycle screaming by at 20-something thousand rpm.

But at vintage races these days, which classes of cars—or bikes— bring you running to the fence? Aren't they ones that pound the ground and hurt your ears? The ones you'd be most scared to drive?

So where are today's equivalents of those great brutes?

Legislated into extinction, mostly. My opinion, again, but generally today's race cars are boring. I'm not saying they're uninteresting, or unenjoyable, or lacking in aesthetic appeal. And they do put on good

Mark Donohue, Porsche "Panzer," at Laguna Seca, 1972.

races. But the cars themselves are so shackled by rules and so tamed-down with technology that they seldom take my breath away.

Officials have always been unnerved by power and speed, and they're forever imposing new limits. To many today, 800 horsepower is too much. Others draw the line lower. I've been in conversation with one sanctioning body figure who is determined to keep his cars under 500 horsepower because "most drivers can't handle any more."

Uh . . . isn't that supposed to be the point? Why would we want to watch somebody doing something anybody can do?

Even when they harbor floods of power, cars today are apt to ration it out. Banning traction control would be one of the few prohibitions I'd support. Pity it takes one party owning all the engines, as in CART, to be sure of enforcing such a ban.

Yes, I can still find forms of motorsport with a wretched excess of horsepower. Sprint cars on dirt leap to mind. So do the top Pikes Peak machines, and also almost any big motorcycle on any surface. In drag racing they have so much power they can't even measure it—whee!

But in most kinds of racing today, the vehicles are just too well-mannered for my taste. I miss the awe I used to feel, and the fear.

How lucky we are to have vintage racing. Bastion of the brutes.

52

F1 Gets MAD

Vintage Racecar, December 2008

GRAND PRIX RACING comes with a new look in 2009. Among other significant technical changes, such as wider cars, grooveless slicks and Kinetic Energy Recovery Systems (think "electric power-to-pass"), there are new aero rules intended to improve a car's ability to overtake another.

Included is this fascinating detail: Front wings will be driver-adjustable for angle of attack. That's right—F1 is getting Movable Aerodynamic Devices.

Well, well, well.

This goes way back for me. Not that they've noticed, but the European politicos and I have been at loggerheads on this for nearly 40 years. It was early in 1969 when F1 regulators hastily slapped a ban on the high, suspension-mounted wings that some teams had only recently started copying from Jim Hall's Chaparrals.

Eventually worded to forbid "moving aerodynamic devices," the ban spread throughout the sport like rot in a bowl of fruit. It even got into my beloved Can-Am, changing and regulating the very shape of what had once been a wild-and-free frontier of unrestricted race car design.

Jim Hall was so disappointed by this clampdown on aero innovation that he quit the Can-Am. For me and for many, a light went out of racing.

The proximate cause of F1's original ban was a pair of nasty accidents suffered by Graham Hill and Jochen Rindt in their Lotus 49s during the 1969 Spanish GP. A few laps into this dash through a city park in Barcelona, first Hill and then Rindt experienced identical failures of their strut-mounted rear airfoils.

Hill, the reigning world champion, escaped his mighty crash with minor injuries. Two laps later at the same place, Rindt—who evidently did not slow much through the accident scene—had his rear wing buckle in the same way. He slammed into the wreckage of Hill's car, and had to put in some hospital time.

From his bed, Rindt wrote a famous open letter calling for wings to be removed completely. One of his arguments was that airfoils created turbulence that robbed the following car of downforce, thus inhibiting close racing.

The FIA's response, handed down mid-practice at Monaco two weeks after Barcelona, was a half-measure: downforce-devices would still be allowed, but only within certain dimensions; they had to be part of the bodywork or fixed to it, and they could not move or change angle while the car was being driven. This sketches out the basic race car we've watched in most series ever since.

Besides Jim Hall (and myself), Porsche was another party disturbed by this ruling. That year's slippery new 917 Le Mans coupe could no longer use its original suspension-linked hinged tabs that were meant to keep it stable at its very high speed. It took some big accidents and a lot of inspired development testing before that car became raceable.

To me, listening in on all the various aero debates over the years, I've sensed an almost theological element. It's not that people failed to recognize the inherent power of aerodynamics before Jim Hall started harnessing it. Downforce-inducing wings were explored on speed record cars in the 1920s (by Opel) and 1930s (Mercedes).

But in 1955, when Swiss engineer Michael May appeared at the Nürburgring with an airfoil mounted above the cockpit of a Porsche Spyder, shocked officials refused to let him race it.

It blocked other drivers' vision, was one reason given. A few years later at Indy we would hear the same nonsense about the Turbine's shimmering exhaust. Some people said the real problem with May's wing was that this lowly privateer was lapping faster and looked smarter then the factory team.

I suspect May's wing and later ones violated an ingrained aesthetic sense, perhaps even a religious conception, about "what an automobile should be." We all claim to like innovation with our racing—but we don't like too much of it too fast!

Consider that officials tend to be of an older generation than hot young race car designers. Someone who came into the sport in love with the svelte sports racers of the 1950s, say, might well have seen the angular, bewinged, vastly faster machines of the following decades as monstrosities. "Automobiles are not supposed to be aeroplanes!" was surely a cry that echoed down the corridors of power.

Honestly, I feel a tendency to such sentiments myself, and I remember it took time for me to see the beauty in the Chaparrals and other winged cars.

But not embracing continuous evolution would condemn us to watching the same old spec cars year after year.

Oh, wait . . . we are.

Back to wings. Although some earlier race car bodies appear to have flirted with downforce at the front, rear-end lift was a little-understood problem until 1961, when American driver Richie Ginther, formerly an aircraft mechanic, put what he called "a trim tab" on the back of a Ferrari prototype. More widely known as the "ducktail spoiler," it swept racing, often over objections by some who groused that "what it spoils is the looks." They were no happier about the "chin spoilers" that came along later to nail down the front ends.

Jim Hall took the next big step in 1965, when he developed a pivoting spoiler low on the rear bodywork of his Chaparral 2C. By pushing what looked like a clutch pedal (it wasn't; his GM-built manual transmissions had torque-converters rather than clutches) he could trim the spoiler flat for less drag on the straights. The 2C won its first race.

A year later, on a developed version of the same chassis renamed the 2E, Hall and friends at Chevrolet combined that idea with mounting an airfoil on pylons rising from the rear suspension uprights. That sent the downforce directly to the wheels, bypassing the chassis, which meant the springs didn't have to be extra-stiff to carry the additional load.

Supple over the bumps, a leech in the turns and bullet-fast on the straights, Chaparral's 2E was usually the fastest car in 1966 Can-Am qualifying, and Phil Hill headed a team one-two at Laguna Seca.

If Colin Chapman didn't see pictures of that system then, he certainly would have in 1967, when Chaparral's 2F enduro car with the same strutted airfoil won at England's Brands Hatch. In mid-

Pete Lovely, winged F1 Lotus 49, at Donnybrooke, 1969.

1968, the Lotus 49 appeared with its own version. At the end of that year, Graham Hill clinched the championship in Mexico driving a 49 that even had a fourth foot pedal to feather the wing angle.

So far so good, but Chapman was a notorious stretcher of engineering envelopes. He made his wings bigger and bigger, and at Barcelona in 1969 he got too greedy. As is well-documented in Michael Oliver's book, *Lotus 49: The Story of a Legend*, Chapman sent both Hill and Rindt into the race with modified, untested wings too flimsy for the forces they generated.

What Lotus lacked, compared to Chaparral, was Rattlesnake Raceway, Jim Hall's private test track literally out the door of his Texas shop. But neither did Chapman, an undeniably brilliant innovator, exhibit Hall's methodical, patient approach to the unknown. In the middle of a hectic GP season, Chapman did his development at race meetings. At Barcelona, he tried it in the race itself.

The consequence of this near-disaster was a knee-jerk regulatory response that outlawed not poor engineering, but an entire nascent technology.

For four decades, drivers have been stuck in cars with rock-hard rides and "aerodynamic sweet spots" far narrower than necessary. Countless fans have been robbed of good races because cars couldn't be fine-tuned to changing conditions without a pit stop. Never mind the street cars with self-adjusting aerodynamics; racing's mental doors were shut.

Why, after so long, is F1 getting MAD back? Because, finally, science has been involved in the rulesmaking. Despite insisting in public that there's nothing wrong with difficult overtaking, behind the scenes F1 bosses have had a formal Overtaking Working Group devising fixes. On www.grandprix.com, Joe Saward tells the whole story; look for "Insight—Applying science and commonsense to overtaking."

Basically, the 2009 regulations narrow and elevate rear wings (which remain fixed), while lowering and widening those on the front. The purpose is to let a car follow another more closely without losing so much downforce.

Simulations indicated, however, that the following car will still be unstable. Thus its driver can crank in more front wing angle—though only through a maximum of six degrees, and only once per lap (controlled by F1's spec ECU).

So it's a very small scrap of freedom. But let us rejoice in it. Aero is no longer evil.

Since I ranted about the above, F1 has decided driver-adjustable front wings didn't help with overtaking and replaced them with driver-adjustable rear wings, which do help, a little. It all seemed so much simpler in Chaparral's day.

53

Man or Machine?

Vintage Racecar, March 2009

You KNOW HOW someone's opposing opinion, one that seems inconsequential enough to let slide at the time, can keep gnawing on you till finally you just gotta explode?

That's what I've been nursing ever since a NASCAR telecast last year, when I heard announcer Darrell Waltrip say something like, "C'mon, guys! What the car is don't matter. This is a people sport!"

Three-time Cup champ DW, aka "Jaws," is an expert and entertaining stock car commentator, and I'm happy to learn from his knowledge and give due consideration to his views. His many views.

But this one makes me scream.

Alas. I seem to scream against the hurricane of history. Those of us—I cannot be alone, can I?—who love racing machines for their own intrinsic and individualistic beauty, and who enjoy technical diversity on our starting grids, face ever stronger forces that are driving the sport toward homogenized cars, and therefore trivialized cars.

NASCAR's all-but-all-alike Cars of Today? Let's not even bother complaining about them. IRL is even worse, giving us nothing but one engine in one chassis, with bodywork rules so tight that, as one Indy car engineer dryly told me, "They leave just enough open to us so we don't complain too much." Formula 1 is rapidly trending the same way.

Piero Taruffi, Lancia, at Sebring, 1954.

Spec classes make sense for economic reasons, and I grant that such reasoning is ever more persuasive these days. Certainly in a ladder series, where the object is to nurture talent, it's appropriate that "the car . . . don't matter." In such cases I agree, it is "a people sport."

But not in every case, no sir. Endurance racing would have no meaning if the cars were identical. In recent ALMS seasons, the battles between big diesels and smaller gasoline-ethanol engines has brought new excitement to the prototypes, while having multiple classes makes for spine-chilling traffic.

Also, the whole point of the new "Green Challenge" in ALMS is to stimulate competition between manufacturers toward future power technologies. (I love that Corvette was the first winner. What a way to sell your spouse on letting you get a ZR1. "See, honey, it's *really efficient!*")

Long-distance racing also requires more than one driver per entry. It rather dilutes any "the driver is our star" marketing premise if there's two or three or even four names on a roof. "The number seven driver, he's my favorite. Uh, who is he right now?"

Lately I've been covering off-road racing, where you still see a fascinating variety of vehicles. Body shapes, engine types and positions, suspension solutions . . . all are free in the desert, or at least way more free than anywhere else in these strictured times.

The way racing was, creative minds could stretch the envelope. Envelopes now are pretty much unstretchable.

This rant; it's all the fault of my upbringing. When racing first interested me, a big part of the appeal was the fantastic variety of fascinating cars. Going to a sports car race was like visiting a wild animal park. Jaguars, Cheetahs, Prancing Horses . . . exotic, thrilling, ever-novel stuff.

And the pace of development was so giddy. Before my eyes, in a scant few years, front-engined bullets transformed into mid-engined downforce devices. Steel chassis became aluminum monocoques, and then suddenly there were composites. I witnessed turbos being harnessed. I saw cars with multiple engines and others with six wheels. Electronics, hydraulics, fuel chemistry once ran riot.

Production classes were interesting, too, because they were real cars, not tube-framed pretenders. As I watched Austin Healeys and Alfa Romeos competing against MGs and Porsches and Triumphs, I'd watch closely to see which seemed to handle the best; that's the one I'd daydream about having.

Today, who can tell? Even the least modified of production cars are so stiffened with roll cages and laden with ballast that their track behavior can be scant guide to their road manners.

No wonder all these rules-happy racing bodies talk up the drivers. They've made the cars so dull, drivers are all they've got to sell.

Sorry, people are only half of racing's equation. It isn't balanced without soul-stirring machinery. And while I may *admire* a driver, I simply cannot accord him—no, not even her—the frank love I feel for a 250F Maserati or a D-type Jag.

Dammit, I *need* great cars!

There, I feel better. Especially now that I've read that three-time Cup champ DW cherishes a personal collection of cars he used to race.

Must be they do matter.

54

When Indy was Awesome

Vintage Racecar, January 2011

A COUPLE OF YEARS and a bit ago I suggested in this spot that, during these times of economic stress, Indy car racing might be rejuvenated by reviving the old stock-block engine idea of Formula 5000. A variety of production-based engines work well in Grand-Am, giving the technical diversity that genuine motorsports enthusiasts love and making those stubby little coupes interesting, at least under the engine covers.

I meant that as a stop-gap, until things pick up and the Indy industry can get back to *real* racing motors.

Naturally, nobody listened to me and instead Indy car fans are "looking forward" to a new generation of V-6s that will be pure-bred racers but all alike, performance-controlled and sound-muted by turbochargers.

Much the same lies in our F1 future.

What a thrill.

I guess the problem I have as an old-timer is that the olden times spoiled me. When motor racing first captured me, it was the motors that did it. My dad would take me to Bridgehampton and Lime Rock and Sebring, where I would see and hear the most astonishing racing machines with the most awe-inspiring engines: jewel-like fours and sixes, thundering eights, screaming 12s, even astoundingly intricate 16s.

As a young road race fan, I didn't have much interest in Indy racing—until suddenly the Europeans I so admired invaded the Speedway. Almost overnight, the same old, same-old Roadsters with their four-bangers up front gave way to mid-engined modernity.

Abruptly, my pit lane prowl for technical diversity expanded from, look, so-and-so has slightly repositioned his Offy to, wow! The Lotus with its four-cam Ford is *fantastic!*

That Gasoline Alley day in 1964 when I first witnessed Jim Clark's DOHC V-8 warming up was a life-changer. Visually, the thing was daunting, a feast of bristling ferocity, all cam covers and jutting inlets and that intricate "bundle of snakes" exhaust writhing from the top.

Mario Andretti, turbocharged Hawk-Ford, at Dover, 1969.

Two men squirted raw fuel down all those injection stacks while a third cranked the starter, and the monster exploded to life. If I didn't actually jump back, I felt an impulse to. As the mechanics warmed it up the old-fashioned way, blipping the throttles, out of the twin barrels of that "pom-pom" anti-aircraft gun exhaust came the most fearsome sounds, a rising, raucous *Brazzz* and then, as the throttles snapped shut, a WHOMP! of excess methanol igniting in the megaphones. *Brazzz*-WHOMP! *Brazzz*-WHOMP! *BRAAAzzzzz*-WHOMP-POMP! Even in bright daylight, you could see muzzle-flashes of flame.

A man strapping down in front of that was a man indeed.

Perhaps that's all I need to say about why so few of today's restricted, emasculated, buttoned-down and hidden-away racing powerplants light my fire. Like I said, I got spoiled young.

Does it have to stay this way? I've heard all the reasoning about cost containment and competitive parity and "racing is no longer about engineering innovation, it's entertainment" but, frankly, I think the wrong people are doing the reasoning.

Let me suggest an analogy from the publishing world. Some years ago a magazine editor whom I admired, and not only because he gave me work, wrote something unflattering about vehicles made by a major advertiser. The automaker yanked its ads. Our publisher yanked the editor.

Well, you may be saying, what did the dope expect? Business is business. It must run smoothly. The magazine can only survive if cash keeps coming in.

To that I say, yes, but who are we publishing the magazine *for?* The advertisers? I propose our true audience is the reader, who I think will appreciate learning that, honestly, a particular vehicle is sub-par.

If we lose our readers, we really will lose our magazines.

In the same way, just as I felt that particular publisher ought to have backed his editor in his service to the readership, it is my opinion that in racing the fans should come first. I see that not being the case these days and, as I look at all the empty seats around race tracks, it appears a lot of fans see it that way too.

Yes, tickets are pricey and the economy is sour. Yes, racing today is a very complex and sensitive global business and teams, manufacturers and sponsors are all dancing atop tightropes. And yes, we're probably past the time of major technological innovation in terms of piston engines, at least, and also car configuration, chassis design, aerodynamics and all the other rapid changes that made the 1960s and '70s so exciting.

But do the businesspersons running today's same-old show sincerely think that chaining down and caging in the once-wild race car beast will retain its intrigue for the enthusiast?

My feeling is that too many series these days seem to be running scared of Public Opinion. They think their race cars have to be Relevant. Economical. Eco-friendly. Environmentally unobjectionable. Just like ordinary passenger vehicles.

But . . . don't we already *have* enough ordinary passenger vehicles? Shouldn't our racing machines be . . . extraordinary? Else, why would anyone want to watch?

Is it really impossible to get back to race cars that make us jump back in awe?

55

Will Future
Race Cars Endure?

Vintage Racecar, February 20! I

SLEEPWALKING THROUGH that great Goodwood paddock of my mind, I delight in thousands of historic racing machines at every hand. All are magnificent and most are momentous, but some few hold my slumbering gaze longer than the rest.

Bugatti 35s ... Alfa straight-8s ... D-types ... GTOs ... GT40s ... 917Ks ... Fangio's 250F ... Gurney's Eagle ... Mario's Lotus ....

Plenty here to love, but this being fantasy, I lift my eyes to a distant corner of the grounds where F1 cars of the future are already gathering. Specifically, ones built to the 2013 regulations announced at the end of 2010. And I wonder: Will any bring a smile to my dreaming lips?

Is it worth my while even to walk over there?

Awakening to a sensation like a dash of cold water, I lie in grey light, pondering somberly: Are the grandest years for my beloved race cars really over?

I fear there's an epidemic of emasculation striking everywhere. In F1, as of 2013 engines will shrink from today's mandatory 2.4-liter, normally-aspirated V-8s to turbocharged 1.6-liter fours which are to be rev-limited to 12,000 (vs. 18,000 right now).

Turbo boost and energy-recovery systems will be governed to keep horsepower at about today's level, the mid-800s as I understand it, but with a 35-percent improvement in gasoline economy and hence carbon footprint. To further foster sustainability, the current limit of eight engines per car per season will drop to five, then to four.

It is hoped this drastic reduction in engine spec will reverse the recent trend of major automakers defecting from F1, making it more attractive to an industry under fire to meet governmental green goals. The thinking seems to be that forcing racers into the mold of road cars is somehow rational.

Last month I indicated how I feel about that. I'm not on board with the notion that the supposed world pinnacle of competition cars has to mirror the congestive mass of production vehicles. To me, racing is all about *breaking free* of the everyday.

However, presented with a load of lemons, one looks into recipes for lemon chiffon pie. Is it at all possible that two years hence I'll check out F1's New Breed of diminutive, turbo-muted four-bangers and see something keen about them?

History: let's look to the luscious lovelies gracing our fantasy vintage paddock. I'll narrow it down to a few of my own favorites and try to discern why they've become immortal in so many of our hearts.

I'll start with the Maserati 250F, the last world championship mount of the illustrious Juan Manuel Fangio. The year was 1957, too early for me to actually witness the great man's feats, but precisely right for words and pictures to imprint him and the car on my soul. Denis Jenkinson, in particular, wrote movingly of Fangio's incredible skill at holding this sensitive, snappy front-engined F1 in opposite-lock drifts down through the esses at Rouen.

The 250F was described as beautifully balanced, a driver's friend, a refined instrument of pleasure that everyone adored. If you longed to experience driving perfection in the mid-1950s, the Maser was the machine you dreamed of.

And it was beautiful. Its lines and proportions were as poised as its performance. From the low bullet prow, up along the smoothly cresting

top line to the fulsomely rounded tail, the car looked to be drawn with a single sweep of a master's pencil. Then the master worked in just the right amount and scale of mechanical texture: the graceful long double exhaust, the sparkling wire wheels, the rows of delicious rivets.

And that engine! An inline-6, meaty dual cam boxes, triple Weber carbs . . . That engine alone deserved a spotlit place of honor in my home.

There had been more powerful cars before the 250F, and many faster ones would come after, but as a timeless example of engineering as fine art, *race-winning* art, I say there are none to beat it.

Although Dan Gurney's Eagle was its aesthetic equal. Body loft lines that sing in your heart, V-12 engine that resounds in your soul, the spiritual satisfaction of knowing that All-American Dan in his American-made car (with English engine) drove to victory against Europe's best.

Jaguar's D-type makes my shortlist, especially in long-nose form with a headrest fin. Protest all you may care to about unenlightened aerodynamics and unsophisticated rear suspension and heavy iron engine block; that means I'll have one in my living room and you won't.

Why does this car so appeal to me? Part of it is its historical importance, a culmination of a time when a small, scrappy company pulled itself out of the ruins of war and re-established Britain's former claim on France's great endurance race.

Historical timing is another; like the Maserati, the "D-Jag" hit me between the eyes just when I was most susceptible to the adventure and drama and beauty of motor racing. I remember being thrilled to hear this Mulsanne missile would go *180 mph!*

And also like the 250F, I relish the contrasts embodied in this petite projectile: the voluptuously curvaceous envelope so densely packed with muscular machinery.

Oh, and the scrumptious Jaguar engine sound!

Lola T70, Aston Martin DBR1, Cobra 289 FIA, McLaren M8B, Norton Manx. . . I could go on, and on, and on. But let's see where we are.

How well do I love F1 cars I watched (on TV) in 2010? What, if anything, will I miss about them come 2013?

Though I'm a nut for engines, I have to take exhaust sound off the table. TV simply doesn't do it justice, and as most of us are unlikely to attend a GP in person, we won't know that turbo-fours restricted to 12 grand are but a thin, reedy echo of what used to be.

When we first heard "turbo" we might have flashed back to the 1,000-horse monster motors of a bygone 1.5-liter formula, but as noted earlier, the Green Machines to come will be regulated to the same performance levels as today. At least that's not a comedown. Today's cars are pretty quick, and if you've been watching, I hope you agree they're pretty entertaining. No, they don't drift like Fangio at Rouen, except by mistake, but you can see the drivers *driving*.

Historical significance? Well, technically minded posters on message boards—I like forums.autosport.com—are saying just wait, you're going to see quantum leaps in powertrain efficiency that will, indeed, benefit everyday vehicles down the road. Whatever.

Pulchritude? I have to say, it took me a few races to get used to the ungainly new wings, jumbo jet in front and Pitts Special out back, but I did get used to them. (Their failure to improve passing as promised is another topic.) As for overall aesthetic appeal, never mind the 2010 Red Bulls won the championships, they quite pleased my eye. I thought they looked snarky.

Two years hence, F1 race cars will be even further shaved, honed, polished, more exquisite in every tiny detail.

No, they're not how I would prefer them. But maybe after all I will stroll over to have a look.

I just won't care if they don't fire one up.

Others have expressed similar sentiments, and subsequent to this column's original publication a groundswell of protest seems to have resulted in a postponement of the new F1 engines to 2014, when they may be 15,000-rpm V-6s instead. Or not. F1 is fluid.

Photography Credits

All photographs by Pete Lyons except as noted:

Ozzie Lyons: page 25, 33, 41, 42, 43, 47, 83, 104, 119, 127, 198, 253

Lorna Lyons: title page

Gerry Lyons: page 229

To see more historic racing photos,
visit www.petelyons.com

petelyons com

If you enjoyed this book, spread the word.

- Go to the book's page on Amazon.com and write a review.
- Like our Facebook page (facebook.com/octanepress).
- Follow us at twitter.com/octanepress.
- Email info@octanepress.com and suggest books you'd like to read.
- And don't forget to check out octanepress.com for our latest books!

About Octane Press

Octane Press is an independent publishing company, created and owned by longtime editor and author Lee Klancher. Our team of authors, editors, designers, salespeople, and more are independent-minded book professionals with more than 100 years of experience making books, and even more restoring, modifying, and enjoying enthusiast motorcycles, cars, tractors, and more. We believe vehicle enthusiasts deserve high-quality publications, and work hard to ensure our books are accurate, attractive, and relevant. We exist thanks to hard work and new technology, and our books are available in electronic forms and strongly supported with our Web site.

We encourage your suggestions, ideas, and corrections. Your input helps us improve our publications and make better ones in the future.

Please send any feedback to info@octanepress.com.

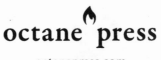

octanepress.com

9386392R1

Made in the USA
Charleston, SC
08 September 2011